A Course in Academic Writing

SECOND EDITION

Renu Gupta

Orient BlackSwan

A COURSE IN ACADEMIC WRITING (SECOND EDITION)

ORIENT BLACKSWAN PRIVATE LIMITED

Registered Office
3-6-752 Himayatnagar, Hyderabad 500 029, Telangana, India
e-mail: centraloffice@orientblackswan.com

Other Offices
Bengaluru, Chennai, Guwahati, Hyderabad, Kolkata
Mumbai, New Delhi, Noida, Patna

First Edition 2010
Second Edition 2017
Reprinted 2019, 2020, 2022, 2023, 2024

ISBN: 978-93-86689-63-4

Typeset in Book Antiqua 11/13 by
Textsoft Solutions Pvt. Ltd

039161

Printed at
B.B. Press, Tronica City Ghaziabad (UP) 201102

Published by
Orient Blackswan Private Limited
3-6-752 Himayatnagar, Hyderabad 500 029, Telangana, India
e-mail: info@orientblackswan.com

Contents

Acknowledgements

For permission to use copyright material, the author and publishers wish to thank:

- Professor Alan Sokal for 'A physicist experiments with cultural studies.' *Lingua Franca*, 62–64.
- Duke University Press for 'Transgressing the boundaries: Towards a transformative hermeneutics of quantum gravity.' by A.D. Sokal (1996) from *Social Text*, 46/47, 217–252.
- Elsevier for
    - R. Gupta (1995) 'Managing general and specific information in introductions.' *English for Specific Purposes*, 14/1, 59–75.
    - R. Gupta (2014) 'Expectations vs. reality: The readability of texts in the primary grades in India.' *Procedia-Social and Behavioral Sciences*, 116, 3916–3920.
- Language in India for
    - R. Gupta (2007) 'Bilingual advertising in a multilingual country.' *Language in India*, 7/4, 1–14.
    - R. Gupta (2009) 'Cross-professional collaboration on eLearning courses.' *Language in India*, 9, 225–238.
    - R. Gupta (2011) 'Faculty perceptions and use of PowerPoint.' *Language in India*, 11/12, 442–453.
    - R. Gupta (2013) 'The readability of English language texts in the primary grades.' *Language in India*, 13, 534–544.
- Taylor and Francis for
    - R. Gupta and V. Saravanan (1995) 'Old beliefs impede student teacher learning of reading instruction.' *Journal of Education for Teaching*, 21/3, 347–360. www.tandfonline.com/10.1080/02607479550038554
    - R. Gupta (2004) 'Old habits die hard: Literacy practices of pre-service teachers.' *Journal of Education for Teaching*, 30/1, 67–78. www.tandfonline.com/10.1080/0260747032000162325
- Wiley for R. Gupta (1998) 'Can spelling checkers help the novice writer?' British *Journal of Educational Technology*, 29/3, 255–266.

Every attempt has been made to trace holders of copyright. Where the publishers have not heard from the copyright holders at the time of going to press, or where in the absence of complete information, it has not been possible to identify the sources of materials used, the publishers would be grateful for any information that would enable them to make appropriate acknowledgement in future reprints/editions of this book.

Preface to the Second Edition

When I first began writing *A Course in Academic Writing* seven years ago, it primarily grew out of my then recent experiences in India, as some research organisations and universities had asked me to teach researchers how to write research reports. Students were unable to grapple with the modalities of writing an essay for international examinations or write research papers for publication. Examining current teaching practices, I realized that the classroom did not equip the learner at the tertiary stage to write for professional reasons.

Seven years later, when I was asked to write for a second edition of this book, I realised that not much had changed in terms of ability of the learner. But what had definitely changed was that there was an awareness of this gap, and there is willingness to acquire the skills needed for academic writing. This was a need-based requirement, as more and more students wanted to publish their papers in international journals for career enhancement. Reputed journals were no longer willing to accept papers not conforming to international norms. So much so, that the University Grants Commission realised this shortcoming and included academic writing as a skill enhancement course in its recently formulated curriculum.

The years between the publication of these two editions has also been a learning curve for me. I realised that the student who is exposed to the conventional school/university curriculum needs more guidance in order to acquire the skills of academic writing. I therefore decided to make the book more student-friendly. I have re-written some chapters much as I would teach them if I were in front of a class of students, by offering concrete examples and using a task-based approach. Illustrative sample writings are also more cross-disciplinary. The hope is that students will be able to practice on a small task and then transfer these skills to their own term papers.

It is a pleasant duty of the author to thank the publisher for their efforts; I would also like to thank Shiny Chakraborty for helping with this edition of the book.

RENU GUPTA
Bangalore
June, 2017

Preface to the First Edition

This book grew out of my recent experiences in India. Some research organisations and universities asked me to teach their researchers how to write research reports, academic papers, and dissertations. As an examiner for international examinations, I found that candidates manage their spoken English and reading tasks well, but do poorly in the writing tasks because they do not use international conventions. And in the corporate sector and government organisations, supervisors want their employees to write clear and direct reports.

When I examined current teaching practice, I found a gap between the type of writing taught in the formal school/university curriculum and the writing required for professional purposes, such as writing essays in international examinations, trying to write research papers for publication, and writing a coherent report. This book has been written to meet the needs of people at the post-secondary stage who are writing for professional reasons.

The book has been designed for three audiences.

1. Individuals who want a single coherent book that teaches advanced writing skills. There are simple explanations (with visuals, where possible), examples, exercises, and answers so that you can learn on your own.
2. Teachers who have to teach an advanced writing course in English. This is usually run as a 60-hour course spread over two semesters, with small class sizes (of 16–20 students), and individual conferences with the teacher. Ideally, students should work with a draft of their own paper, revising it as they encounter new concepts; during the individual conferences, the teacher provides feedback and guidance on the paper. This would be of particular help to students who have to write a dissertation or thesis.
3. Curriculum designers. Most universities in India do not have courses in advanced writing, although these are a standard component of the curriculum in universities around the world. Such a course could be prescribed in the final year of any programme that requires students to write a thesis—at the MA, MPhil or PhD level—or in institutes where students need to write term papers or reports.

The examples I have used are from the social sciences (particularly language teaching) as they do not require specialised knowledge of the subject matter. However, the principles of clear writing remain the same across all disciplines.

I would like to thank several people. The book began many years ago, when Connie Rylance at the Program in English for Foreign Students at Stanford University showed me that there was more to teaching writing than teaching language; it was finished because Mukti Sanyal at Bharati College, University of Delhi urged me to put these ideas in a book. While the book was being written, several people encouraged me because they understood the need for such a book: Professor Deepa Saran at the Department of Business Economics, University of Delhi asked me to teach her students how to write an M.A. thesis; Professor Jacob Tharu from the CIEFL, as always, listened patiently to ideas I threw his way; and Professor Arpita Mukherjee at ICRIER in New Delhi allowed me to try out the material with her research team. I want to thank all my students from whom I learned how to write; their constant 'whys' forced me to evaluate and articulate my prescriptions. I now understand why authors thank their editor; every author needs an editor like Ketaki Bose, who gently but firmly keeps the author on track.

RENU GUPTA
Bangalore

Introduction

If you think that it is difficult to write, you are correct. Of the four skills in language—listening, speaking, reading and writing—writing is considered to be the most difficult skill to learn.

In school, you learned the basics of writing. In the language class, you wrote compositions on topics such as 'Clouds' or 'A scene at a railway station', using 'big' words and complex sentences. Your teacher corrected mistakes in your grammar and vocabulary, and then gave you a grade; hopefully you read the comments and tried to use them in your next composition. At the same time, in other subjects such as history or biology, you had to write long answers or reports where your teacher or examiner was more interested in the accuracy of the facts than in the language.

Life after school is very different. At the university, your subject (or discipline) becomes central, and the English class exists to help you with your subjects. At first, you may find it easy to pass the examinations if they only check basic understanding of facts through problems sets and essays. But the bar is soon raised and instructors expect you to express your opinion. In the sciences and social sciences, you may be given a project and asked to write a report that includes a justification of the method you chose. In the social sciences where you study competing theories, you may have to write a paper that evaluates these theories. You cannot just describe the theories; you have to give your opinion.

However, you cannot just say, "I believe that....". We want the reader to believe our point of view, so we use logic, data, and evidence from the course readings. This is academic writing. The focus is on the strength and logic of your argument, and language is only a tool to help you express this clearly.

Your writing does not stop here. In the workplace, you will find that you have to craft email messages and write reports for internal distribution or for the general public. And if you decide to become an academic, your standing depends on the quality of your dissertation and the number of papers you manage to get published.

Why Teach Academic Writing?

Universities in the UK and the US find that entering students may have good reading skills, but they cannot write well in their subject areas. Students use the style they learnt in school, whereas texts at the university use more formal language and specific conventions to communicate ideas. To fill the gap, most universities offer a specific course that teaches students how to write academic texts. Although this course is usually offered through the English department, it teaches students how to write in their discipline—economics, history, biology, etc. When I teach the course, the students work on a paper or assignment in their core discipline.

What is Academic Writing?

Essays fall into five broad categories.

1. *Narratives* tell a story. They have a setting, characters, plot, complication, resolution, and ending.
2. *Descriptive* essays paint a picture of an object, a person or an experience.
3. *Expository* essays provide information about a topic. You find these on websites like Wikipedia and in encyclopaedias.
4. *Persuasive* essays try to convince the reader of a point of view, usually based on opinion. Think of advertisements as examples.
5. *Argumentative* essays are the academic version of persuasive essays; they use facts and logic rather than opinion.

School concentrates on teaching the first two types of essays—narrative and descriptive. The focus is on saying something interesting and displaying mastery of the language. Students draw on their personal experience and can use the personal pronoun 'I', evocative language, such as adjectives, and exclamation marks. In the real world, we find them in newspaper 'middles'.

> **Example**
> Her answer was a real **damper**! In a single stroke, she whisked away the **fragrance** of roses, leaving me to my **dowdy** pre-occupations.

Academic writing involves argumentative texts. These texts present a logical argument supported by facts, data, and references to experts. They use formal language and a clear structure that is familiar to readers. This style has not come out of thin air. Since the 1990s, linguists have examined thousands of written texts in different settings—published research papers, office memos, reports and examination essays—and in a variety of disciplines. From this, they extracted the main features, and this is what we teach in academic writing.

Using the Book

This book tries to teach you the basics of academic writing. You should realise that readers are getting used to a standard format in texts and if your goal is to be understood, such a format helps you get your ideas across—clearly, fast, and without being misunderstood.

Once you know the basic format, you can modify it to suit your personal style.

There are a few critical requirements for a course in academic writing.

1. *Do the exercises.* If you skip the exercises, you will be able to give a lecture on writing, but you won't be able to write. This is a textbook and not a manual. You can dip into it if you want answers to specific questions, but you will learn how to write only if you read the explanations and work through the exercises.
2. *Be prepared to revise your work.* Your first draft is not your final draft. You have to revise it at least once, with a gap of a few days between the revisions. This is because writing does not happen in one shot. Writers write multiple drafts of their paper in which they re-organise their points and refine their language. When the paper is done, they edit for clarity and style and finally they proofread for spelling errors.
3. *Get access to a computer.* It is easier to revise a paper that has been written on a computer than revising a handwritten paper. At the least, you will be able to re-organise sentences and paragraphs and view the effect of the change. You can also use the grammar and spell checker to clean up the language in your paper. If you have access to the Internet, even on your smartphone, you can check facts and gather information. If you have time, try to learn touch typing; it is much faster than typing with two fingers.

Organisation of the Book

Chapter 1 explains why academic texts use a certain style and describes the basic format of an academic text, which can be used for short or longer texts. Chapter 2 examines three common approaches that students use to write, and suggests a more organised approach. Chapter 3 describes the pre-writing stage—how to gather information for your text and how to avoid plagiarism.

The next four chapters deal with writing at the paragraph level. Chapter 4 shows how information is organised in a single paragraph. The three chapters that follow—chapters 5–7—describe different ways to organise paragraphs; these are called text types.

Next, we go to longer texts. Chapter 8 compares different text genres, such as reports and research papers. Chapter 9 looks at reports and in chapter 10 you will work on a short research paper. Chapter 11 lists the specifications for a research paper and is primarily intended for academics writing research papers. In chapter 12 you will see how to handle oral presentations, which often go hand-in-hand with writing a paper.

Chapters 13 and 14 should be read after you have written a paper. They are designed to show you how to edit your sentences and choose the appropriate words, so that your message is clear. Students have always enjoyed this section because it is not the same old grammar exercises. Pick any section at random and try the exercises.

Enjoy!

CHAPTER

1 The Big Picture

INTRODUCTION

Today, there are books on writing in different professions—business, engineering, journalism, etc.—and they teach specific genres—business memos and letters, laboratory reports, research papers, proposals, and book reviews. The books draw fine distinctions between genres, such as the persuasive letter versus the internal memo. This is confusing and unnecessary because, at the end of the day, all of them follow the same principles; it is only the content that differs. Once you understand the basic principles, you should be able to apply them to any form of modern written communication and tweak them to suit the specific situation.

This chapter is divided into three sections.

- The type of writing that is expected in the sciences and social sciences. You will skim through two student essays and decide which one is better.
- How texts can be structured. We will look at two different ways to organise the information in your paper.
- The structure of an academic text. We will look at the main parts of such a text and the terms used.

WHICH TEXT IS BETTER?

Below you will see two samples of student writing taken from MBA students who were studying in a foreign university. For their entrance examination, they were given a question from the GMAT examination and asked to write an essay. Read the instructions, and then skim through the two student essays to decide which one is better.

Example
In this section, you will need to analyse the issue presented and explain your views on it. There is no "correct" answer. Instead, you should consider various perspectives as you develop your own position on the issue.

"Some people argue that the salaries of corporate executives should be linked to those of their lowest-paid employees. This would improve relations between management and workers, reducing costly labor disputes and increasing worker productivity. What these people overlook, however, is that these high salaries are necessary to attract the best managers, the individuals whose decisions have the greatest impact on the overall well-being of the company."

Which do you find more compelling, the argument that worker and executive salaries should be linked or the response to it? Explain your position using relevant reasons and/or examples from your own experience, observations or reading.

Below are two essays that were submitted by students. I have left their essays intact and not edited even their spelling mistakes. Skim the two essays and grade them on a scale of 1 to 6. The lowest grade is 1 and the highest is 6; a passing grade is 4.5. Here is your grading sheet.

	Grade	Reasons
Student A		
Student B		

Student A

"As certain as death and taxes." If anything else could be included in this oft repeated line, it would be 'high executive salaries'. And it is not for nothing that boards of directors entrust these executives with responsibilities of astronomical consequences, providing them equally astronomical pay packets.

Before we even discuss this further, let us analyse a more pressing issue that has been facing human resource managers lately. Should executives' pay packages be linked to those of their employees?

Proponents of this line of thought need to be aware of many issues that significantly work against the very advantages that they think creating such a link would provide.

Arguing that such a link would reduce the frequency of labour disputes is flawed. Often, such disputes occur because of a plethora of other factors, totally unrelated to the absence of such a link. For instance, as recent as two weeks back, the labour union of a major bank in Italy resorted to a strike because of the lack of security measures for them during the transition to EURO, nothing related to compensation.

Lower level workers in most industries are not concerned about the level of salaries of the executives. They are worried about issues that more directly relate to their subsistence, like those that relate to their shelter, food, education for their children, etc. As long these basic needs are adequately satisfied by their managers (executives), they give their best in their jobs.

Individuals who have been following the boom in management education during the last decade would realise that the boom would not have taken place, had the participants (MBA graduates) not proven themselves in the real business world. It has long been accepted that a good business education imparts the basic analytic, problem-solving and creative skills required to succeed in an executive position. And such individuals succeed because they are able to take their companies forward. Make no mistake, they are able to do so because of the help of their employees. Ford would not have achieved the world-renowned effiency of their assembly lines, had it not been for the dedication of its line workers. PSA at Singapore would not have been the world's no 1 operations organisation, had it not been for the skills of its floor workers.

The boards of directors obviously want their companies to be in the top league. In the realisation that a good leader is essential to do so, they offer ever-growing fat pay packets to attract people with the abilities that have proven to breed success in organisations in the past.

In taking the help of past instances, I do not wish to give the idea that I don't believe in any relation between the salaries of executives and those at a lower level. Because, in the first place, they would not be eligible for such high packages if they were not able to keep their most important assets, their employees happy.

But to impart a solid shape to this tacit link would give rise to a rainbow of issues that would defeat the whole purpose of increasing productivity in the organisation.

Student B

Today some people are arguing that the salaries of corporate executives should be linked to those of lowest-paid employees. They thought that the relationship between two parties would eased and improved. Furthermore the costly labour disputes will be reduced significantly with the worker productivity being increased much.

In my opinion, now the performance of a company is more and more related to the leadership and management shilled owned by a good manager or CEO. There is a old saying that a stock of sheep headed by a lion can beat a flood of lions headed by a sheep. In 21st century the core competence of a company results much from how the corporation leader is managing the people in the organisation because just as Jack Welch, the former CEO of GE said, the people is the most important and crucial competetive tool in the new economy. So the good compensation plan should be offered to attract the excellent executive managers to join and lead the company.

On the other hand, I think that the high level officials in the company should pay enough attention the income gap existing between the managers and ordinary employees. Actually in some company the morale of the employees is very low just because of low payment. In this case the managing team should educate the staff and try make them know that their benefit is linked very closely with the performance of the company which in turn relies so heavily on the conduction of the organisation's executives.

In conclusion, the corporate executives should be paid much more than the employees since they are bearing more responsibilioties and exerting more efforts than the employees, and the actions taken by executives are giving significant impact on the well-being of the company.

Reactions of Teachers

I asked a group of English teachers to rate the two essays. They all agreed on how to rate specific aspects of the two essays.

Item	Student A	Student B
Vocabulary	Advanced	Simple
Grammar	Complex sentences	Fairly simple sentences
Length of the essay	Longer	Shorter
Easy to read	No	Yes
Answers the question	No	Yes

However, the teachers disagree on which essay was better. The Indian teachers graded Student A higher because his language was more complex (vocabulary, grammar, and length of the essay). However, the only foreign teacher in the group pointed out that Student A does not answer the question. She was right; in the GMAT exam, Student A would fail, whereas Student B would pass. The reason is very simple—Student B's English is more basic, but the essay is easy to understand and it answers the examination question.

Straightforward Writing

Why is it better to write in a straightforward way? In academia, there is a famous hoax called the Sokal Affair or Sokal's Hoax. A physicist called Alan Sokal wrote an article in the area of Cultural Studies, which he submitted to a journal, *Social Text*, and it was published. The problem is that the entire article was nonsense. Below we give you one paragraph from Sokal's article. Don't worry if you don't understand what he is saying—you are not meant to!

> Sokal, A.D. (1996). 'Transgressing the Boundaries: Towards a Transformative Hermeneutics of Quantum Gravity.' *Social Text*, 46/47, 217–52.
>
> There are many natural scientists, and especially physicists, who continue to reject the notion that the disciplines concerned with social and cultural criticism can have anything to contribute, except perhaps peripherally, to their research. Still less are they receptive to the idea that the very foundations of their world view must be revised or rebuilt in the light of such criticism. Rather, they cling to the dogma imposed by the long post-Enlightenment hegemony over the Western intellectual outlook, which can be summarised briefly as follows: that there exists an external world, whose properties

> are independent of any individual human being and indeed of humanity as a whole; that these properties are encoded in "eternal" physical laws; and that human beings can obtain reliable, albeit imperfect and tentative, knowledge of these laws by hewing to the "objective" procedures and epistemological strictures prescribed by the (so-called) scientific method.

In a later article, Sokal revealed his hoax, and explained why and how he had done it.

> Sokal, A.D. (1996). 'A Physicist Experiments with Cultural Studies.' *Lingua Franca*, 62–64.
>
> I decided to try a modest (though admittedly uncontrolled) experiment: Would a leading North American journal of cultural studies—whose editorial collective includes such luminaries as Fredric Jameson and Andrew Ross—publish an article liberally salted with nonsense if (a) it sounded good and (b) it flattered the editors' ideological preconceptions?
>
> `http://www.physics.nyu.edu/faculty/sokal/lingua_franca_v4/lingua_franca_v4.html`

The answer, unfortunately, is yes.

In other words, if you have nothing to say, use big words. Or, as we say, if you can't dazzle them with your brilliance, 'baffle them with big words'.

However, if you have ideas that you want to communicate, use simple words and a direct style. In this book we assume that you have something to say and we show you how to do this efficiently and effectively.

Two Types of Texts

There are basically two ways to structure a text—indirect and direct. The difference lies in where the main point is stated. The two texts below are identical except for one thing—the main point of the memo, which is in bold type, comes at different places in the text.

Indirect text	Our investigation shows that the manufacturing processes at Basic plants are outdated. The management is centralised and out of touch with both the market and employees. As a result, sales have dropped and employees are not highly motivated. **It makes little sense to invest in Basic until its processes and management have changed.**
Direct text	**It makes little sense to invest in Basic until its processes and management have changed.** Our investigation shows that the manufacturing processes at Basic plants are outdated. The management is centralised and out of touch with both the market and employees. As a result, sales have dropped and employees are not highly motivated.

Indirect Texts

In indirect texts, the reasoning is presented first and the main point comes at the end. There are various names for such a text—inductive paragraph, indirect order, etc. It is used in the following cases:

1. To give bad news. When rejecting an application, we start with the reasons and then go on to give the bad news. This cushions the blow.
2. To persuade. In business, when you have to persuade a new or reluctant client, lead them gently to your point.
3. Some English proficiency examinations. A few examinations that want to test proficiency in English, such as the University of Cambridge 'A' Levels, ask students to write an essay on a general topic, such as the following:

   "Science and religion will always be in conflict." Discuss.

   Students are expected to present both sides of the argument and then evaluate the better option based on the evidence.

Direct Texts

In direct texts, the main point is stated first and then the evidence to support it is presented. There are various names for such a text—deductive paragraph, direct order, etc. It is used when the information is important. Hence, it is used in business, research in the sciences and social sciences, and any texts for a US audience.

This type of text is both easy to write and easy to read. In writing this text, you merely have to list your points, organise them and present the evidence to support your claims. Readers also find such texts easy to read; they can locate the main point at the beginning of the text. If they want details, they can read further; otherwise they move on.

This book focuses on direct texts because these are used in academia—for term papers, research papers, dissertations, and reviews—as well as in business and engineering—for memos, letters, and reports.

Who wants such texts?

When I taught business communication, Indian students asked in surprise, 'Do people actually write like this?' But one student did say, 'The supervisor at my Indian company wrote in this way—and he was considered to be a very good writer.' Student B, who is from Mainland China, described her essay as 'childish'. In her first language—Mandarin—sophisticated argumentation (as in an indirect text) is taught and rewarded. Another Chinese student explained the strategy she uses to write in English: 'In Chinese I write in many different ways. But in English I use only this direct style of writing. It is easy to follow so I can focus on my language instead of struggling with the different sections.'

Surprisingly, such a 'simplistic' structure is required in several contexts.

Examinations for the US

Since this direct style of writing has come from the US, it is not surprising that examinations for US universities rate such essays very high. These are examinations such as the SAT, TOEFL, GRE, and GMAT. In fact, ETS, the organisation that conducts most of these examinations, developed a software program called Criterion that explicitly identifies the first sentence of each paragraph and checks whether it contains the keywords.

Examinations for the UK

The International English Language Testing System or IELTS is an entrance exam for study in countries such as the UK, Australia, and New Zealand. There are no specific instructions on how to write an essay for the IELTS; however, the current IELTS website stresses that the candidate should address the question and not include irrelevant material.

Corporate sector

In the corporate sector, no one has the time to read elaborate prose; in fact, the preferred mode is a PowerPoint presentation with five bullet points. Business communication is direct; a study by Zaidman (2001) that compared the communication between Israelis and Indians found that Israelis were exasperated by the Indian tendency to use flowery prose and digressions.[1]

ACADEMIC TEXTS

You can see the structure of a basic direct text in Figure 1.1. It has an introduction, body, and conclusion. These three sections are sometimes described as 'This is what I will say. Now I am saying it. This is what I have said.' It seems like a lot of repetition, but it helps readers—they can read any section to get the main idea and skip the other sections.

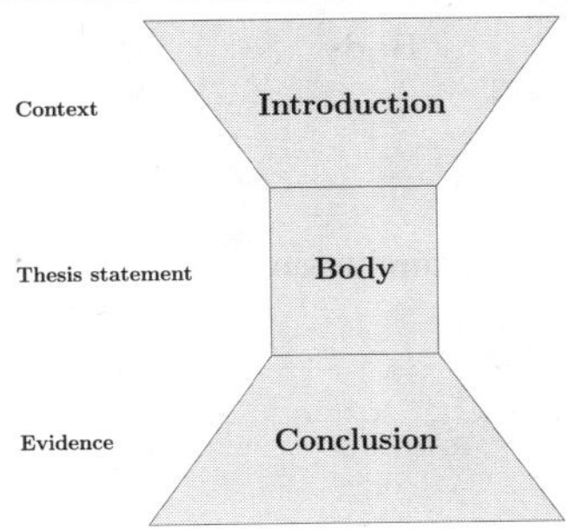

Figure 1.1: Basic structure of a text

[1]Zaidman, N. (2001). Cultural codes and language strategies in business communication: Interactions between Israeli and Indian business people. *Management Communication Quarterly*, 14, 3, 408–11.

This is also called the *5-paragraph essay* because it has one paragraph each for the introduction and conclusion with three paragraphs in the body. A more derogatory term for it is the 'hamburger essay' because the meat or facts are in the body of the essay.

What happens when you write short texts of a page or less, such as a memo or an email message? The introduction and body are essential, but the conclusion is not necessary. Your text will look like Figure 1.2. In longer texts, such as reports, research articles, dissertations and proposals, you will add sections, but the central section remains the same (Figure 1.3).

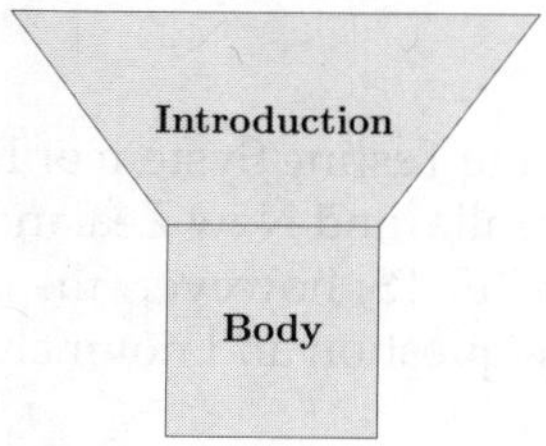

Figure 1.2: Structure of a short text

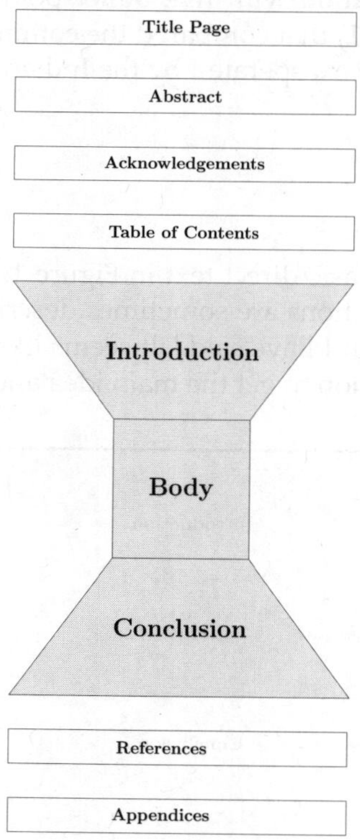

Figure 1.3: Structure of a long text

Sections of an Academic Text

An academic text can be divided into three sections.

1. **Introduction.** The introduction does two things: it states what you will do and why you will do it. This is structured as follows:

    - Provides a context. It explains why the topic is important.
    - Gives a thesis statement. This is a one-sentence summary of your main point.

2. **Body.** In the body of the essay, you provide points to support your thesis statement or main point.

    - The body of the essay consists of paragraphs.
    - Each paragraph describes only one point.
    - The first sentence of each paragraph is a topic sentence that states the main point of the paragraph. The rest of the paragraph provides supporting details.

3. **Conclusion.** The name is a misleading. It implies *therefore* or *QED*, suggesting that it is the end of the argument. However, the conclusion here is merely a goodbye, and so it is a chance to remind the reader of the main point.

    - The conclusion is optional. It is not necessary in short texts, but it is used in longer texts because the reader may have forgotten the main point.
    - It summarises your argument.
    - It does not introduce any new points or ideas. There should be no surprises.

Let's see how this works in a short essay. Look at the notes in the left column and the italicised sentences in the text.

Classrooms for Today

Introduction Main point or thesis statement states the number (3).	With globalisation, English has taken centre stage. The increasing use of English in the business sector and higher education has led to a demand for English proficiency courses in India. However, the current English curriculum in schools and universities is still driven by the English Studies approach designed in the 19th century to impart values to Indians through the study of English literature. *This approach is being replaced by curricula and teaching techniques that focus on language.* Below, *I describe three characteristics of these new classrooms.*
Point 1 Topic sentence	*First, the classes are learner-centred.* There is an old joke about the surgeon who said, "The operation was a success though the patient died." Likewise, in the classroom the issue is not how well the teacher taught, but whether the students learned.

	Rather than selecting tasks, such as a reading passage that interests them, teachers need to view activities from the perspective of the learners —"Is it culturally unfamiliar to the students? Is it related to their current or future situations?" The syllabus has to be designed keeping in mind the entry level of the students, their interests, and the end-point they wish to reach. Within these constraints, the teacher decides on a reasonable goal and designs activities to achieve that goal.
Point 2 Topic sentence	*Second, language is used for communication and so it should be taught for communication.* Students are usually taught to produce grammatically correct sentences, but not how to respond in a conversation. Natural interaction can be set up through scenarios where the participants have different goals.
Example	For example, a student has bought a CD but finds the incorrect CD in the case; the student wants a refund but the store manager prefers an exchange. The interaction between the two parties involves negotiation and responding in real time.
Point 3 Topic sentence	*Finally, classrooms have to be technology-enabled.* Although technology is viewed as a luxury in Indian classrooms, many students and teachers have access to the Internet, which has a wealth of resources for teaching and learning.
Example	In addition to grammar and pronunciation exercises, students can obtain information for writing tasks from sites such as Wikipedia and use concordance programs to examine the specific contexts in which words occur.
Conclusion Reaffirms main point	These features define the classrooms of today, enabling them to help learners acquire proficiency in English. If we do not incorporate them in our classrooms, we risk losing our students to institutions that do.

Terms that We Use

We used several terms above that may not be clear. Let's briefly look at these terms here. We will deal with them in greater detail in Chapter 4.

Thesis statement

You should be able to state the main point of your essay in a single sentence. This sentence is called the thesis statement and is the final sentence of the introduction. The reason for such a short summary and its location is that it gives the reader a map or framework to understand what follows.

Paragraph

What is a paragraph? Students told me that their teachers advised them to start a new paragraph when the text becomes too long. However, that is not the purpose of a paragraph. A paragraph contains only one idea with information to back it up; if you begin moving to a new idea, start a new paragraph.

Topic sentence

If each paragraph has one idea, ideally it should also have a sentence that sums up the main point of the entire paragraph. Such a sentence is called the topic sentence. This sentence can be placed in different positions—at the beginning, in the middle, or at the end of the paragraph.

For readers, the most helpful location is the beginning of the paragraph. This way, the topic sentence provides a map or framework for the information that follows. If the paragraph is very long, the topic sentence may be re-stated at the end as well, but in slightly different words.

Supporting details

To support your claims, you need to provide evidence. These are called supporting details. In the text , the author supports her point with an example.

> Natural interaction can be set up through scenarios where the participants have different goals. For example, a student has bought a CD but finds the incorrect CD in the case; the student wants a refund but the store manager prefers an exchange. The interaction between the two parties involves negotiation and real-time responses.

Transition signals or signalling devices

Paragraphs and sentences are not random but are linked to one another. We use signalling devices or transition signals to indicate these links. The text above uses second to show how this paragraph is linked to the thesis statement and the other paragraphs. Within a paragraph, you can also indicate links by using words such as *however, for example,* and *also.*

EXERCISES

Q1. Find samples of question papers for international examinations, such as TOEFL, GRE, GMAT, and IELTS; their official websites usually have sample answers or suggestions on how to write. You could also try commercial websites and books, but be careful because the testing bodies do not endorse these. Often the material is what the writers think the testing bodies want.

In the suggested answers, look at (a) the last sentence of the introduction, (b) the first sentence of each paragraph, and (c) the final paragraph. How similar are they to the essay given above? If there are no sample answers, read the suggestions carefully.

Q2. Collect samples of short texts from another domain—say the corporate sector. These could be memos, official email messages, executive summaries of reports, etc. You can ask a friend for these samples (if they are not confidential) or find them on the Internet. Look at the structure (not the content) of these texts. How far do they follow the structure described above?

CHAPTER 2 Approaches to Writing

INTRODUCTION

When faced with a writing task, many people start writing immediately, putting down whatever comes to mind. This approach is driven by time-bound examinations, where we have limited time to display everything we know and remember. The reader (usually the teacher or the examiner) has to pick out the relevant information from a jumble of sentences.

Over the past 30 years, there have been two important developments in writing. First, we can now use computers to write texts; this allows one to cut or move text so that the essay is organised better. Second, standards have gone up because examinations and organisations expect you to use this technology. In some examinations, candidates have to compose their essays on the computer and time-bound examinations are giving way to take-home assignments and projects, such as reports and theses. There is now no excuse for a poorly organised text. An essay that resembles a stream of consciousness is no longer acceptable; you are expected to give thought and care to your paper and produce a polished product that is reader-friendly.

In this chapter we look at some approaches used to write texts that are a hangover from the past. Then we will look at two ways to structure a text.

WAYS OF WRITING

You have to write an essay, a term paper, answer an examination question, or write a thesis. How do you go about filling the pages? Here are some methods that are commonly used. All these approaches assume that your first draft is what you will submit as your final version. Composing on the computer, on the other hand, allows you to revise your paper.

Begin at the Beginning

In the book, *Alice in Wonderland* by Lewis Carroll, the King advises Alice on how to tell a story: 'Begin at the beginning and go on till you come to the end: then stop.' You can see this approach in the example below. For a take-home assignment in history, this was the question:

> **Question**: Discuss the factors that were responsible for the rise and popularity of Buddhism in India.
>
> One student began his essay this way.
>
> Buddhism appeared in India around 250 B.C. and the person responsible for the founding of Buddhism was Buddha. The simplicity of Buddhism in comparison to Hinduism, the role played by Asoka and the political and economic reasons were responsible for the rise and popularity of Buddhism.
>
> Buddha was the son of a chief of the Sakyas, a small tribe in the Himalayan foothills. He became an ascetic and went in search of the knowledge that would liberate man from sorrow.

All the students in the history class considered this an appropriate introduction for a history assignment. However, the history professor ran his red pen through the entire introduction, saying that it was unnecessary—the student should assume that the reader already knows these facts and begin directly with a discussion of the factors.

The problem is that many students spend a lot of time writing and polishing the introduction. Their teachers may have told them that the introduction is critical—it should capture the reader's interest and draw the reader into the essay, or that the examiner forms an impression of the essay from the introduction. So, students work hard on the introduction. Then, in the time and space that remains, they hurriedly address the main points they want to make.

Why is this a problem? The introduction is meant to be just an introduction—a 'hello, here are my points.' For this reason, most readers skip the introduction because it is merely a hook on which the argument is hung. Equally important, proficient writers usually write the introduction last, after they have finished writing the body of the paper. So, spend most of the time you have on the body of the paper rather than on the introduction.

The solution is simple. Don't think in terms of the time you have, whether it is three hours or five days. Instead, think in terms of the amount of space you have been allotted—say, 500 words—and you will realise that your introduction has taken up 300 words.

Throw in All Your Thoughts

In time-bound tests, there is no time to organise facts; so, writers throw in information as it comes into their heads. There is also no time to edit at the end. Even if the writer wants to re-organise the essay, editing a handwritten paper will turn it into an illegible mess. A similar problem can be seen in newspaper columns that have a fixed length; if the article is too short, peripheral information may be added to make it longer.

Below is the introduction to an essay written by a university student. In this text, a few words (marked in bold) have been used repeatedly.

> Language is a **system** of **communication**. It is **communication** by word of **mouth**. It is the mental faculty or power of **vocal communication**. It is a system for **communicating** ideas and feelings using **sounds,** gestures, signs or marks. It is the code we all use to express ourselves and **communicate** to others. Any means of **communicating ideas**, specifically, human **speech**, the expression of **ideas** by the **voice** and **sounds** articulated by the organs of the throat and **mouth** is a language. It is the systematic **communication** by the use of **sounds** or conventional symbols. This is a **system** for **communication**. A language is the **written** and **spoken** method of combining words to create **meaning** used by a particular group of people.

This text is a collection of random sentences woven around the words *communicate, human, speech, sounds, ideas, system,* and *meaning*. If you re-arrange the sentences in a different order, it does not affect the text. The reader knows as much about language in Sentence 10 as s/he knows in Sentence 1, and there is no progression or development of the point. This text is often seen in timed examinations where students try to 'fill up pages'.

Chaining

In chaining, the writer elaborates on new information as it comes in. Here is a text that shows how the ideas progress.

> The trees on campus should not be **cut**. If we **cut** them down, we lose an enormous **variety** of trees. This **variety** ranges from *kikar* to *amaltas* and represents the **biodiversity** of the region. **Biodiversity** is now recognised as important for the planet to avoid **global warming**. We see the signs of **global warming** in....

As the writer ends one sentence, s/he elaborates on the information that has been introduced. Gradually, the writer moves away from the original point, namely, that the trees should not be cut, and it becomes difficult to return to this point. In this style of writing, the text is driven by words and phrases instead of the ideas.

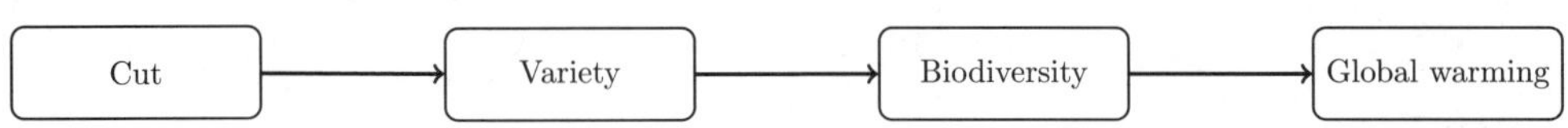

Figure 2.1: Chained sentences

Balanced Versus Weighted Essays

There are two ways to organise your essay: by presenting a balanced view or by directly stating your position.

Balanced Essay

One method of writing an essay is to present both sides of an argument. This is preferred in exams that test your written English skills, such as university examinations. You are given a controversial statement and asked to discuss it.

For example, in a topic like 'Science and religion will always be in conflict', you are expected to present both sides of the argument; at the end of the essay, you can remain neutral or opt for the more convincing argument. Your essay would look like Figure 2.2.

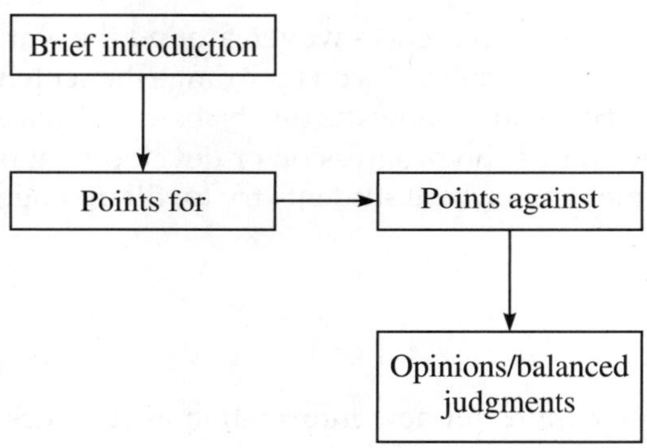

Figure 2.2: Structure of a balanced essay

Such an essay requires a sophisticated writer and an equally sophisticated reader. The writer has to present equally valid points for both sides of the argument, which requires wide reading. This type of essay is a favourite with examiners because it requires breadth of knowledge.

However, consider the burden on the reader. The reader has to follow the argument step-by-step until the end, when the writer's stand is revealed. This works if the reader has fluent reading skills and the leisure for the task. However, information requirements have changed. Today, the emphasis is on speed of information retrieval. Also, since information is readily available through the Internet, the focus has shifted to the author's point of view.

Weighted Essay

In Chapter 1, we have used a sample text on Classrooms of Today. This text is organised as a hierarchy and can be diagrammed as shown in Figure 2.3.

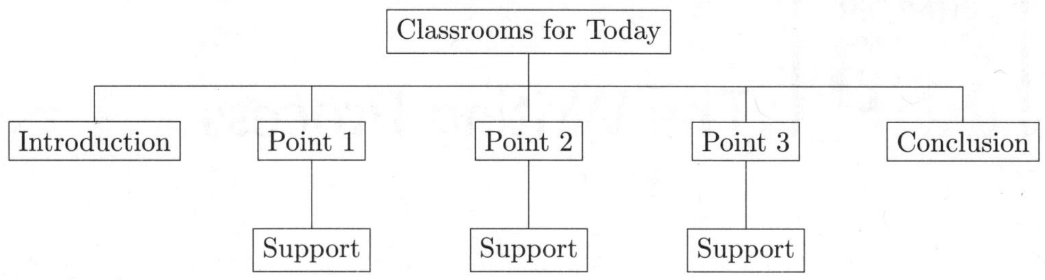

Figure 2.3: Hierarchical organisation of a text

EXERCISES

Q1. Find one of your recent essays and think about the following:

a. Which method did you use?
   - Begin at the beginning
   - Throw in all your thoughts
   - Chaining

b. Why did you use this method?
   - I was short of time.
   - The teacher wants a long essay.
   - This is the way I always write; I don't know any other method.
   - I didn't use a computer.

c. If you were asked to re-do the essay, what would you do?
   - Gather more information
   - Correct the spelling mistakes and grammar
   - Write more neatly
   - Make the essay shorter
   - Make the essay longer
   - Re-organise the paragraphs
   - Improve the first sentence

Q2. Peer review: Swap essays with a partner and give suggestions on the structure (not the language) of the essay.

CHAPTER 3 The Writing Process

INTRODUCTION

An essay or a paper requires information—facts, figures, examples, etc. In closed book examinations, you must remember and recall such information, and you are rewarded for your memory. But at the university and later, the focus shifts from remembering information to presenting an argument supported by evidence from research papers that you find in the library or on the Internet. This opens up a vast universe of information, but it also throws up new problems.

1. How do you find and select the information you need? This part of the writing process properly comes under the skill of reading. You need to have fluent reading skills if you want to write.
2. The 'facts' differ in the material you find. Which research findings are correct? You will need to critically examine and evaluate the information.
3. If the information is available to everyone, what should I write?

This chapter goes through the main steps in the writing process. To do this, we will pick up a general topic: *Noise pollution*. The three main steps are:

1. Brainstorming for ideas and creating an outline.
2. Gathering information from sources. This involves—
   (a) Evaluating the quality of sources.
   (b) Avoiding plagiarism.
3. Sorting the material—
   (a) Skimming and revising the outline.
   (b) Taking notes.
   (c) Re-writing the material using quotations, summaries, and paraphrases and acknowledging your sources.

From this, it should be clear that writing is not a one-shot effort. It requires time and frequent revisions. It is better to use a word processor, because otherwise you will have to write your revisions by hand.

Brainstorming and Outlining

The first step in writing a paper is to jot down your ideas. This is called brainstorming. It does not matter if you have very few or very simple ideas, because you will add to them as you read. Next, organise your ideas into groups and you might get something like Figure 3.1 for the topic noise pollution.

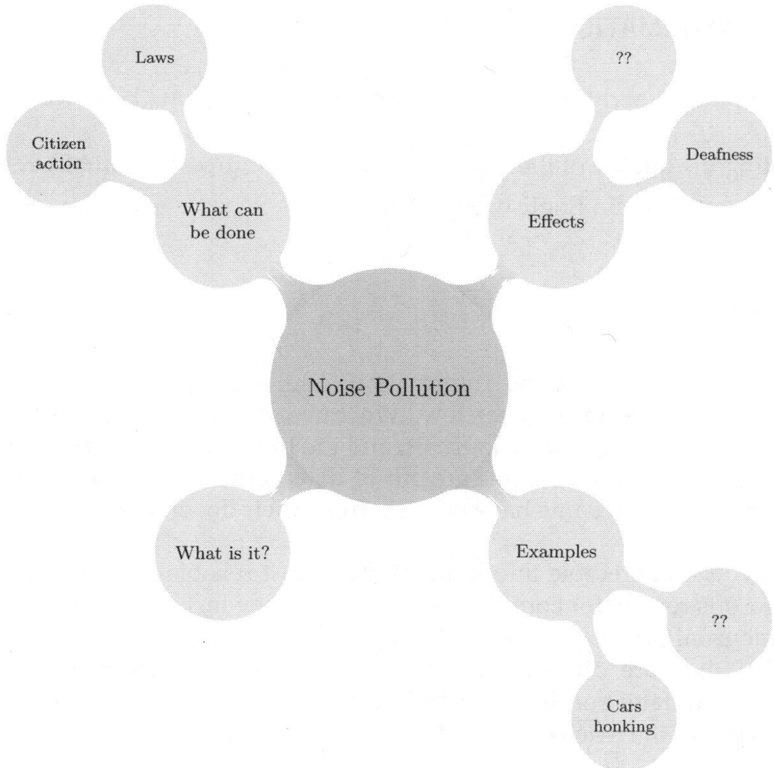

Figure 3.1: First outline

Notice the features of this outline. First, we use only phrases and not complete sentences; if you begin writing sentences, you will get lost in the language and lose the thread of your argument. Second, the outline is tentative; some points have question marks because you may not find the evidence for it. You can re-arrange the points later, dropping those that do not work and adding others as you do your reading or thinking. Keep this outline in front of you—above your desk or at the beginning of your paper, so that you can refer to it as you write.

For a long paper such as a report or dissertation, PowerPoint works very well. You can put only a limited amount of text on one slide, which stops you from writing complete sentences (and paragraphs). Write your thesis statement and main points on different slides; this helps you see the structure of the document clearly.

Next, you need to find more information on the topic. For this, you will have to go to the library or check the Internet. But here is the important part. The information you find will widen your knowledge of the topic, but your basic argument should remain the same. You will use the information to support your argument. So, you include the sources of the information as if to say, 'This is not just my opinion; many respected people say the same and here are their names'.

GATHERING INFORMATION

The second step in the writing process is gathering information. Here we encounter two issues.

1. Evaluating the quality of the information. Not all sources are equally reliable.
2. Plagiarism or, in plain English, copying.

Evaluating Sources

We're lucky that we live in the Information Age, where information is no longer controlled and available to a select few. We can get the information we need from television, newspapers, magazines, journals, and the Internet. But is it that easy? Different web pages tell different stories. Some are out-of-date, some do not know their facts, some have their own biases, and some have not proofread their documents.

So, where do you find credible information? The most reliable sources are those that go through a rigorous review for content and language. They include printed encyclopaedias and referred journal articles; however, their rigorous review process can take a year or longer, so that they are often out-of-date by the time they are printed. Commercial databases are up-to-date, but like encyclopaedias and journal articles, they are extremely expensive and out of the reach of even libraries, let alone students.

The answer seems to be the Internet. But you need to check whether the sites are reliable. Anyone and everyone is writing on the Internet—giving their (unsubstantiated) opinions, promoting products and themselves, and writing tributes. The use of adjectives is a giveaway: if the piece has a lot of glowing adjectives, you have hit promotional material or a fan site and if the adjectives are negative, the writer is using the Internet to air his or her personal grievances.

The solution is to begin with a fairly reliable site such as Wikipedia. From there, you need to track all the references, and read the original papers to check the facts.

Avoiding Plagiarism

Plagiarism is copying other people's work and passing it off as your own. This can range from copying sentences and paragraphs to copying entire papers. The Internet has made it easy to both find and copy material; in fact, websites have begun copying from one another and you find identical paragraphs on multiple websites.

What does plagiarism look like? Look at the two texts below, which are taken from two novels.

Megan McCafferty *Sloppy Firsts* (2001: p. 7)	**Kaavya Viswanathan** *How Opal Mehta Got Kissed, Got Wild and Got A Life* (2006: p. 14)
Bridget is my age and lives across the street. For the first twelve years of my life, these qualifications were all I needed in a best friend. But that was before Bridget's braces came off and her boyfriend Burke got on.....	Priscilla was my age and lived two blocks away. For the first fifteen years of my life, those were the only qualifications I needed in a best friend....But that was before freshman year, when Priscilla's glasses came off, and the first in a long string of boyfriends got on.

Source: Wikipedia. http://en.wikipedia.org/wiki/KaavyaViswanathan

Because Viswanathan's text is so close to the original, it sank her literary career.

The Internet is a great source of information. It is also a great resource for copying paragraphs and even entire papers. It is tempting to copy and paste information you find on the Internet and turn it in as your own work.

If this is your strategy, think about why you do it. Which of the following apply to you?

1. My English language skills are weak.
2. The original text says it better than I can ever hope to state it.
3. There is no difference between copying from the Internet and reproducing an essay from a *kunji*, except that it is faster to copy-paste than to type.
4. Material on the Internet is free for anyone to use. I can download music and movies. So, why not download papers?
5. The term paper carries only 5 marks, so why should I put in any effort?
6. The paper is due tomorrow and I have no time.
7. I don't know how to write a paper, because I was never taught how to do so.

Reasons 1–3 are common among East Asian students for whom English is a foreign language. One Japanese student told me that the one thing he learned from my writing class was that I didn't care how bad the English was but the paper had to be written in his own words. Another Japanese student was indignant when told that he had copied his undergraduate thesis from another student's thesis; he said, 'I didn't copy it—I spent 8 hours typing it in!'

Reasons 4–7 are more common in India. The perception that material on the Internet is free for anyone to use is so rampant that even commercial organisations copy material from websites and try to pass it off as their own. The Internet is viewed as a giant wastepaper basket in the sky that everyone can dip into.

The main reason why students and researchers copy work is that they have never been taught how to write a paper—how to select relevant information, express it in their own words, and use it to build an argument. The rewards for doing original work are so small that many people think that is not worth the time and effort of learning how to do the work. Just go to the Internet and get what you want.

How easy is it to spot plagiarised material?

Very easy! If you can use the Internet to copy material, I can do the same to find your source. If I have any suspicions, I type a few words from a student paper into Google and the original paper pops up. Software such as SCAM and companies like *Turnitin.com* match a student paper against other papers to check how much has been copied.

People try to circumvent this by using synonyms and inserting a few errors so that the software does not detect the copy. But you don't fool teachers; in a disorganised essay, a logical paragraph in brilliant English stands out. We now have plagiarism detection tools that match the style of different paragraphs in an essay—and can detect who wrote which section of the essay.

How much can you copy?

There is an old joke that if you copy from one source, it is plagiarism, whereas if you copy from two sources, it is research. But how much can you copy from someone else's work? The rule of thumb is not more than 10 consecutive words can be copied.

Some material does not have to be acknowledged because everyone knows it. Everyone accepts that the sun rises in the east and that language is a system of communication. These are accepted facts and broad concepts that you need not acknowledge. But if you got specific ideas and examples from another source, you have to re-write it in your own words and acknowledge the source.

What are the consequences of plagiarism?

If you are caught plagiarising, it can be extremely embarrassing for you. A long string of famous people have written theses or books that have plagiarised material from other works. Plagiarism became an issue in India in 2015 when international journals pointed out that several Indian scientists had copied their data and papers from other publications. Now, Indian universities are required to use plagiarism detection software on all dissertations that students submit.

Most teachers do not want to take the trouble of confronting a student with plagiarism, so one can get away with it for a while. But in academic settings, plagiarism is regarded as a serious offence and can lead to a lower grade, a failing grade, or even suspension. First, there is a copyright issue. Someone else has put a lot of time and effort into researching and writing the material, so copying their work amounts to stealing; this is like copying images and songs from the Internet and selling it as your own material. The second reason has to do with the purpose of academic work—when you write an assignment or research report, you are graded on your views and ideas. If you submit an assignment lifted from other sources, the original author deserves the grade, whereas you get a zero—or worse.

The bottom line is: Read widely and give credit to your sources.

Sorting the Material

Once you have found some material on your topic, what do you do with it? This is where many students get stuck. They take sentences or paragraphs from here and there and try to assemble it into a text. The result is a patchwork of random sentences that doesn't make sense even to the 'author'.

Look at the material you found on noise pollution. How much of it can you use? When I did a search, I found numerous 'canned' essays that say nothing; you can do better. Also, much of the material says the same thing in different words because they have copied from one another. In such a case, choose the original or the most coherent article, and drop the rest. This will reduce the volume of material.

Next, step back from the material. You will get demoralised or lost if you read the brilliant work done by other writers. Then, follow these three steps in drafting your paper.

1. *Skim through the material and revise your outline.* Skim through the copied material to become better informed about the topic and to gather support for your arguments. Revise your outline.
2. *Take notes.* Read some material carefully and note down points you can use.
3. *Re-write the material and acknowledge your sources.* Paraphrase, summarise or quote the material you have chosen in order to provide support for your argument. Then, list your sources in the references. This way you avoid the charge of plagiarism; you also give weight to your arguments by showing that you have done your reading and some authorities on the subject hold the same view.

Skimming and Revising Your Outline

Once you have your outline, you can begin looking at the material you have downloaded or photocopied. Your purpose is to extend your knowledge about the topic and to see what material is available. You may have to revise your outline as you come across new information or find that no information is available. Read rapidly, not carefully. Skim through the texts to get the overall idea. Here's how it works:

1. Read the title and subtitle(s), if there are any.
2. Read the first sentence of all the paragraphs.
3. Read the whole of the first and last paragraphs if the piece is long.

Try to read the text below. By doing this, you will be skimming the text. The information in the text also tells you how to skim a text.

In the Information Age, we are bombarded with information from all sides. To sift through this information, we need to read quickly and efficiently. For this, we use a technique called skimming. In skimming, we read only select portions of the text. What are these portions? The first paragraph usually provides an overview of the text, so read it carefully.

Sometimes the first paragraph is merely a 'warming up' or too general to give you an idea of the gist. In this case, read the second paragraph too. Now you have some idea of the text, so you do not need to read every paragraph.

Don't read every word or every sentence .... take in .... key words.

The first sentence of each paragraph contains the main point ... the rest is supporting detail .... skip.

In addition to the main point, try to get specific facts .... names dates .... numbers

Don't be afraid to leave out half or more of each paragraph ....xxx .... xx ....

Don't get interested and read everything ....

If the text is long, look at the organisers .... headings sub-headings .... illustrations graphs ....

Once you get the main points, you can always go back and read the text more carefully .... read details .... evaluate the facts

We use skimming for numerous texts ...... reports ...... newspapers ...... blogs

Read the final paragraphs carefully. These usually summarise the main points. Note that skimming is useful to get an overview of the text.

Now that you have some information on your topic, you should go back to your outline and refine it. You may need to delete some ideas because you could not find information, or include ideas that came up in your reading. Your revised outline may look like the following.

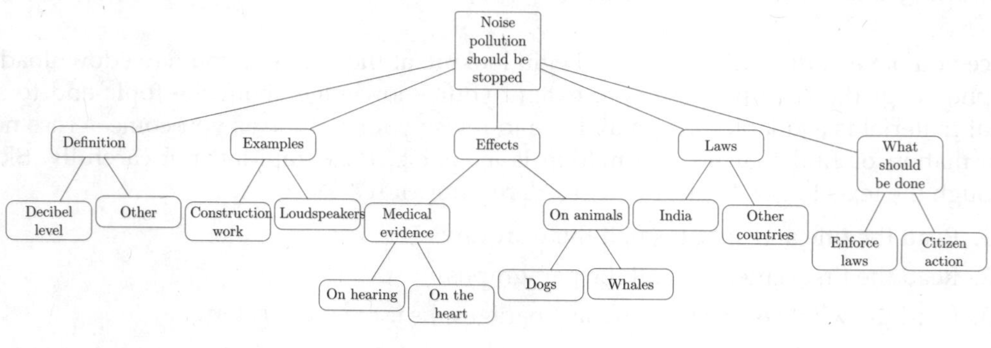

Figure 3.2: Revised outline

Taking Notes

Once you have identified a few useful articles, read them carefully and extract the main points. There are two ways to do this.

1. Highlight the most important point in each paragraph. If the text is written clearly, this will usually be the first sentence of the paragraph. You can either use a highlighter or write the main point in the left margin.
2. Diagram the information. Students find this strategy very helpful when they have to extract information from technical or dense texts. Below is a paragraph from a research paper. To understand this material, you can create a diagram like Figure 3.3.

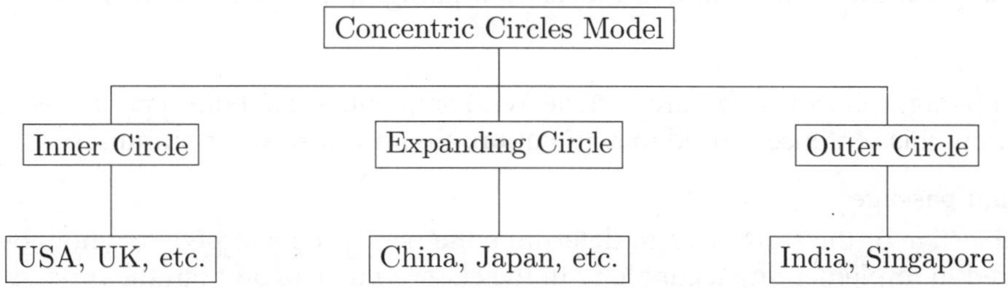

Figure 3.3: Diagram of content

> One useful framework for examining bilingual advertising is the Concentric Circles model of the spread of English (Kachru, 2005). In this model, countries in the Inner Circle (such as the US, the UK, Australia, and Canada) use English as their first language, whereas in the Expanding Circle, English is primarily a foreign language as is seen in China, Japan, Taiwan, Thailand, Russia, etc. Countries in the Outer Circle, such as India and Singapore, fall between these two groups, because in these countries English is "used as an institutionalised additional language" (Kachru 2005: p.14).

Re-write the Material

If a text provides support for your argument, you may want to include the information in your essay. It is critical to acknowledge the sources from where you obtained the information. This helps you avoid the charge of plagiarism as well as lends credibility and weight to your argument.

There are three ways to include material in your text.

Quotation

These are the *exact* words from the source and are placed within quotation marks. You cannot change the words or punctuation marks. You should give the source and the page number where the quotation appears. Quotations are useful for definitions and if you intend to argue against someone's opinion. Avoid long or numerous quotations because they give the impression that you are 'filling up the pages'.

Paraphrase

In a paraphrase, you re-write the original sentence in your own words.

Summary

A summary captures only the main ideas in a paragraph or text. Again, use your own words.

Here is a paragraph from a research article, with one sentence in bold type. Below that you can see how this sentence is used in a quotation, a paraphrase and a summary.

Original passage

One objective of the study was to determine the perceptions of people who would be involved in implementing technology in the classroom. The pivot in the process is the classroom teacher; in the teaching of writing, it is the English language teacher. We designed a questionnaire to assess teachers' perceptions and use of computers. The questionnaire was distributed in 24 schools and 127 English teachers responded. **The results show that although school teachers have access to computers, they use them for limited purposes and many are not comfortable using them**; for instance, 53% of the teachers said that they are afraid of the computer (page 92).

Source: Gupta, R., Hvitfeldt, R. and Saravanan, V. (1998). 'The use of computers in the teaching of writing.' In S. Gopinathan, A. Pakir, Ho Wah Kam, and V. Saravanan (eds) *Language, Society and Education in Singapore* (pp.91-104). Singapore: Times Academic Press.

Quotation

In Singapore "….although school teachers have access to computers, they use them for limited purposes and many are not comfortable using them". (Gupta, Hvitfeldt, and Saravanan 1998: p.92)

Paraphrase

In Singapore, computers are available in the schools, but teachers use them for a few tasks and the majority are not confident about using computers. (Gupta, Hvidfeldt, and Saravanan 1998)

Summary

Although computers are available in Singapore schools, teachers make limited use of them for teaching. (Gupta, Hvidfeldt, and Saravanan 1998)

Paraphrase: In other words

We use paraphrase in everyday life, when we explain what we mean during a conversation.

- The planet that we inhabit is spherical in shape. *This means that the Earth is round.*
- Your Customer Service was excellent; it was a bad idea to change it because with the new procedure it takes 30 minutes to talk to an agent. *If it's not broken, why fix it?*

Paraphrasing helps you include ideas in your text in your own words. You use it when you want to present evidence that either supports your argument or that you will refute. When you write a long paper, it is useful to paraphrase your own words. For example, the abstract, introduction and conclusion present similar material and it is boring for the reader to see the same sentences in different sections. If you know how to paraphrase, you can present the same material in different words.

A paraphrase can be as long as the original sentence or text, but the wording and sentence structure must be different. All those synonyms that you learnt in school come in useful here. And, of course, you must make it clear that this is not your own idea but another person's work.

Summarising: In short

In a summary, you briefly present the main ideas of another text in your own words. Summarising is often taught and tested as a standalone technique; we see this in competitive examinations that include a precis writing task. Book reports and reviews include a summary of the material before providing the evaluation. A summary is much shorter than the original text; it can even be only one sentence. It captures only the main ideas, omitting details such as examples and explanations.You should use your own words. Do not lift phrases from the original text. Check that you have not copied more than 3 or 4 consecutive words from the original text. When you summarise an article, do not give your opinion. The evaluation should remain separate from the summary.

Acknowledge your sources

As you identify material that you can use, begin creating a list of references. This goes at the end of the paper. It will help you keep track of your reading. It also establishes that you have done some serious reading and are not 'writing off the top of your head'.

You are now ready to start writing paragraphs that expand and explain the points in your outline.

EXERCISES

Q1. Using the Internet or other resources (such as dictionaries or encyclopaedias), find the following information. You need to hunt for the correct information because several sources give partial or incorrect information.

1. What is the national language of India?
2. Is India north or south of the Equator?
3. Which metal is extracted using the Bessemer Converter?
4. What is the difference between the words *grateful* and *thankful*?

Q2. The abstract of a research article is given below. Create a diagram that summarises the information.

Abstract
The prevention and detection of plagiarism has become an educational challenge because students and faculty can easily copy material from the Internet. Numerous plagiarism detection software (PDS) tools are available, but they draw on different technologies and models. This study evaluates two commercial PDS tools in terms of their speed and accuracy. LINE uses substring analysis to identify matches in a string of words, whereas SCUM uses Bag of Words analysis to identify words that are common to two texts. The results show that LINE returns results faster, but is less accurate than SCUM because it does not take synonyms into account.

Q3. The sentences below have been taken from a single text. As the first step in paraphrasing, replace the words in italics with synonyms. (The second step would be to change the sentence construction.)

1. Although *infants* are able to *discriminate* colours, the ability to name the basic colours appears *at a much later age*.
2. This study *looks at* children's ability to perceive colours and name them.
3. Children in pre-school and elementary school were asked to *choose* the odd colour in a set of four colours, and to name a colour.
4. The results *reveal* that children in pre-school can *perceive* colour differences, but colour names develop with age.
5. The results show a developmental *order* in the acquisition of colour terms.

Q4. Write a one-sentence summary of the passage on acquiring colour terms.

Q5. Select one of the topics below (or find your own topic) and create an outline. The outline should only consist of phrases.

1. The most liveable cities in India
2. Using technology effectively in the classroom
3. Recycling waste is not a waste of time
4. Climate change is a hoax
5. Challenges faced by women in the workplace

ANSWERS

1. 1. India does not have a national language. Most websites state this correctly.
   2. India is north of the Equator. Most sites talk around the point. You can deduce the answer if you look at a map of the world.
   3. This is a curious case. In school textbooks and entrance examinations, the Bessemer Converter is used to extract copper. In real life, it is used to extract iron and steel.
   4. Most sites describe *grateful* and *thankful* as interchangeable words. However, if you go to http://www.english-test.net/forum/ftopic2030.html you see the correct answer:

      Grateful means that you appreciate what someone has done for you and you want to express your thanks. *Thankful* means that you are relieved/ pleased that what you hoped for has happened.

      Example: She was grateful to her teachers and also thankful that she had passed her exams.

2.

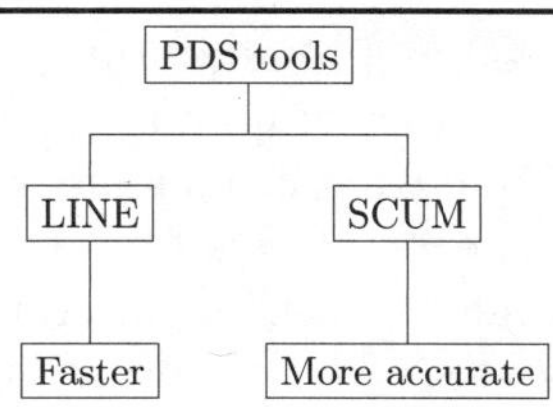

Figure 1: Diagrammed information

3. 1. Although *babies* are able to *differentiate* colours, the ability to name the basic colours appears *when they are older.*
   2. This study *examines* children's ability to perceive colours and name them.
   3. Children in pre-school and elementary school were asked to *select* the odd colour in a set of four colours, and to name a colour.
   4. The results show that children in pre-school can *see* colour differences, but colour names develop as they grow older.
   5. The results show a developmental *sequence* in the acquisition of colour terms.

4. The study found that there is a developmental sequence in the acquisition of colour terms.

CHAPTER 4 Writing a Paragraph

INTRODUCTION

In this chapter, we will look at how to write a paragraph. A paragraph such as the following is an information dump that is difficult to understand.

> In India, there are over 40,000 fuel retail outlets, with only 2,000 belonging to private companies. The private companies are Essar, Reliance, and Shell. BPCL, HPCL, IBP, and IOC have a market share of 80 per cent. The market share of private retailers has been affected by the fixed prices for domestic fuel and the lack of government compensation for the price subsidies. Most of the LPG and all kerosene is sold by government oil companies.

When you write well-connected sentences in a paragraph, you are not far from writing a good essay. Here is the text we will work with.

> **Sample Paragraph**
>
> In order to understand the scope of the problem, the government decided to conduct a survey of the schools in the area. The survey found several problems with the schools in the area. Nine schools were identified—six primary schools and three secondary schools. Through school visits, teacher interviews and classroom observations, data was collected and the findings submitted as a report to the government. The survey was conducted during the school year—from July to March—when teachers and students would be available. Teachers were frequently absent and, when they did appear, their teaching was of poor quality. Most of the schools had no electricity. Many teachers do not have adequate qualifications; while most have a BA degree, they do not have a teaching certificate. There are no sports facilities and students spend the break in the classrooms. Some schools did not even have separate rooms for the classes. Teachers complained that many students do not buy textbooks. In winter, the lack of electricity means that students cannot read their textbooks or see what they are writing.

There are a few key elements in writing a coherent paragraph.

1. One paragraph should contain only one idea.
2. The sentences should be arranged in some order.
3. There should be a topic sentence.
4. The supporting details should follow the topic sentence.
5. Irrelevant information should be deleted.
6. A concluding sentence can be added.

We will now work our way through these six steps, using our text as an example.

One Paragraph, One Idea

A paragraph should contain only one idea. If there are two ideas, write two paragraphs, or you will confuse the reader. The sample text is about problems in schools, but there are two distinct ideas: how the survey was conducted and the findings of the survey. This is shown in Figure 4.1.

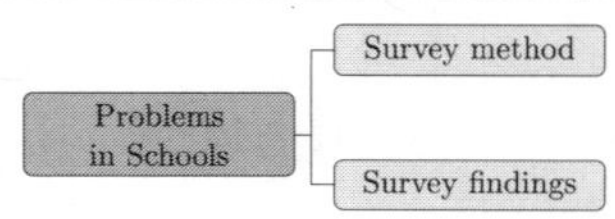

Figure 4.1: Basic outline of the sample text

Organise the Information

Next, we organise the information. We put each piece of information under the appropriate heading. You can see this in Figure 4.2.

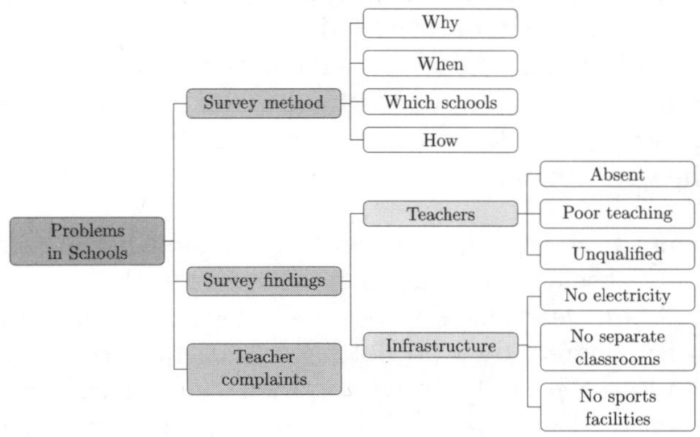

Figure 4.2: Detailed outline of the sample text

Delete Irrelevant Information

From the detailed outline in Figure 4.2, we see that one piece of information does not seem to fit. The sentence is "Teachers complained that many students do not buy textbooks." Since it destroys the unity of the text, delete the sentence. We now get Figure 4.3 and the text looks like this:

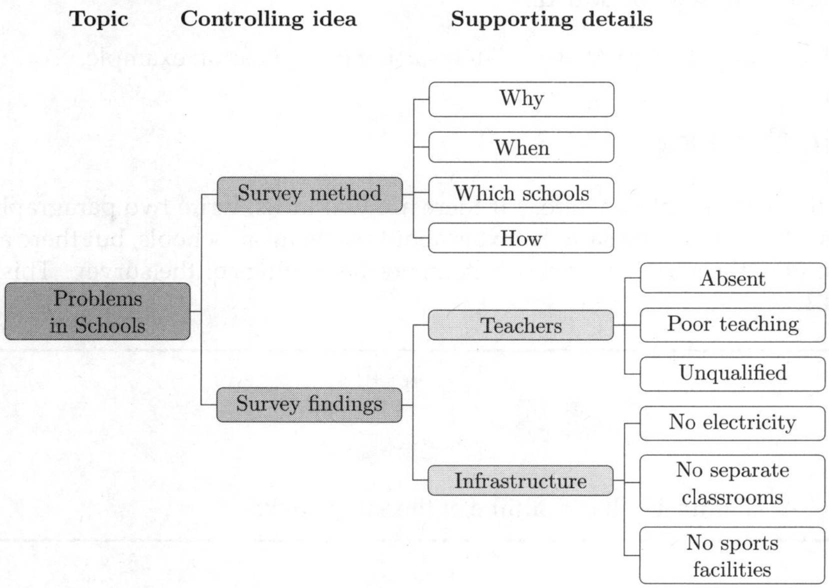

Figure 4.3: Modified outline of the sample text

In order **to understand** the scope of the problem, the government decided to conduct a **survey** of the schools in the area. The survey was conducted during the school year—**from July to March**—when teachers and students would be available. **Nine schools** were identified—six primary schools and three secondary schools. Through **school visits, teacher interviews and classroom observations**, data was collected and the findings submitted as a report to the government.

The survey **found** several problems with the schools in the area. **Teachers** were frequently absent and, when they did appear, their teaching was of poor quality. Many **teachers** do not have adequate qualifications; while most have a BA degree, they do not have a teaching certificate. Most of the schools had no **electricity**. In winter, the lack of **electricity** means that students cannot read their textbooks or see what they are writing. Some schools did not even have separate **rooms** for the classes. There are no sports **facilities** and students spend the break in the classrooms.

Write a Topic Sentence

Every paragraph is about something. This is the topic of the paragraph and can be found in a keyword that is repeated. Look at the first two sentences of our sample text. Since the word *survey* is repeated, the reader knows that the topic of the paragraph is *survey*.

> In order to understand the scope of the problem, the government decided to conduct a survey of the schools in the area. The survey was conducted during the school year.

Parts of the topic sentence

The paragraph could be anything about a survey: the method, the findings, the expenses, etc. So, we have to limit the scope of the paragraph. This is done through a topic sentence. The topic sentence has two parts—the topic and the controlling idea.

- The topic states the theme of the paragraph. It is usually a keyword.
- The controlling idea limits the topic to a specific aspect that will be discussed in the rest of the paragraph.

The government conducted a survey of the schools to understand the problem.

↑ Topic: The government conducted a survey of the schools

↑ Controlling idea: understand the problem.

Location of the topic sentence

The topic sentence is usually placed at the beginning of the paragraph; this helps the reader by acting as a guide. The rest of the paragraph provides details to support the main idea.

Topic sentence	In order to understand the scope of the problem, the government decided to conduct a survey of the schools in the area.
Supporting details	The survey was conducted during the school year—from July to March—when teachers and students would be available. Nine schools were identified—six primary schools and three secondary schools. Through school visits, teacher interviews and classroom observations, data was collected and the findings submitted as a report to the government.

To summarise,

- The topic sentence is usually the first sentence of the paragraph.
- The topic sentence helps the reader by acting as a guide or map.

- The topic sentence helps you write the paragraph. Once you have a topic sentence, it is easy to fill in the supporting details.
- The topic sentence should not be too general or too specific. If it is too general, you won't know what to include or exclude. If it is too specific, you have nothing left to say or write.

Now, let's look at the second paragraph of our sample text. It has no topic sentence. Here is the content of the paragraph. Level 1 is the topic, Level 2 is the controlling idea, and Level 3 gives the supporting details. From this outline, it is easy to write a clear topic sentence that has a topic and a controlling idea.

The survey found problems with both the teachers and the infrastructure.

↑ Topic (survey found) ↑ Controlling idea (the teachers and the infrastructure)

Add Supporting Details

After you have stated your main point in the topic sentence, you need to back it up. Supporting details lend credibility to your claims by providing evidence, explanations, statistics, facts, examples, etc. Supporting details merely back up the topic sentence and do not introduce new ideas.

Notice how this is done in Paragraph 2 of the sample text.

Topic sentence	The survey found problems with both the teachers and the infrastructure.
Evidence: Teachers	Teachers were frequently absent and, when they did appear, their teaching was of poor quality. Many teachers do not have adequate qualifications; while most have a B.A. degree, they do not have a teaching certificate.
Evidence: Infrastructure	In terms of infrastructure, most of the schools had no electricity. In winter, the lack of electricity means that students cannot read their textbooks or see what they are writing. Some schools did not even have separate rooms for the classes. There are no sports facilities and students spend the break in the classrooms.

Write a Concluding Sentence

How does one end a paragraph? In long paragraphs, we usually restate the topic sentence in different words to remind the reader of the main point. We do not introduce any new ideas here, since that would make it a new paragraph.

A suitable concluding sentence could be written as this.

> *From the findings, the main problem areas in schools are teachers and inadequate infrastructure.*

EXERCISES

Q1. In each paragraph below, the sentences need to be put in the correct order. Put them in the correct order by numbering them.

Paragraph 1

1. This makes it cost-effective for advertisers.
2. In this mode, companies send advertisements to a mobile phone using SMS (short messaging service).
3. The latest marketing tool is SMS advertising
4. However, advertisers are being careful, because such users may find these advertisements intrusive.
5. Unlike television and print, people tend to read messages on their mobile phones.

Paragraph 2

1. The experiment, called 'The Hole in the Wall', is now being replicated in other Indian cities.
2. Studies show that children do not need teachers to learn how to use a computer.
3. Within days, the slum children had taught themselves how to surf the net, and download games and music.
4. A group of researchers in Delhi placed a computer in a wall next to a slum and watched what happened.

Paragraph 3

1. So, this everyday phenomenon is an important source of information for linguists.
2. Linguists take such errors seriously because they show how the human mind works.
3. When a person says 'sums up' for 'thumbs up', we dismiss it as a slip of the tongue.
4. For example, when 'speech production' comes out as 'preach seduction', it shows that the speaker already plans to use the word 'production'.

Q2. The paragraph below contains unnecessary information. Underline the sentence that does not fit.

> An increasing number of mobile phones users are browsing and searching the Internet on their handsets. The Internet was originally set up in the 1970s for defence purposes. However, mobile users face four problems. The first two problems are obvious: the small screen size makes reading difficult and it takes forever to type text. Despite advances in technology, connectivity and downloads are slow. Finally, web pages are designed for larger screens and would have to be redesigned for mobile phones.

Q3. In the paragraph below, underline the topic sentence. It may not be the first sentence in the paragraph.

> The university has introduced technology at all levels. However, the use of technology varies widely across departments. There is heavy use of technology in the sciences, particularly in computer science. The social sciences come next, where computers are used to store and analyse data. The humanities merely use technology to videotape lectures and stream them to students.

Q4. For the paragraph given below, select an appropriate topic from the options.

1. Many people are surprised to learn that dinosaurs could be both very large and fairly tiny.
2. Dinosaurs were massive creatures that roamed the earth.

The biggest creatures to walk the earth were the Sauropod dinosaurs. They could weigh about 70 tons and were often taller than four-storey buildings. There were other species, like the Paralititan, that were even bigger and could have been over 100 feet long. Though large, both these groups were mainly plant eaters and quite peaceful. By contrast, dinosaurs like Compsognathus were as small as chickens but they were nimble, fast-running, crafty meat-eaters.

Q5. In the topic sentences below, identify the topic and the controlling idea and underline them. Write T for the topic and C for the controlling idea.

1. It is clear that most college graduates today are familiar with technology.
2. Through the ages, linguists have studied how languages work
3. How history is interpreted depends on the time and the ideology of the historian.
4. Our habits and feelings often seem to hinder our writing.

Q6. Write a concluding sentence for the movie review below.

> The new movie *Twits* is showing in cinemas this week and has been advertised as a movie for the whole family. The plot is simple enough for twits: two friends arrive in the big city where they have a series of (mis)adventures involving the underworld, girls, gangs, and more girls. The plot is non-existent, but the furious action and stunning locations try to make up for it.

ANSWERS

1. **Paragraph 1**
The latest marketing tool is SMS advertising. In this mode, companies send advertisements to a mobile phone using SMS (short messaging service). Unlike TV and print, people tend to read messages on their mobile phones. This makes it

cost-effective for advertisers. However, advertisers are being careful, because such users may find these advertisements intrusive.

Paragraph 2
Studies show that children do not need teachers to learn how to use a computer. A group of researchers in Delhi placed a computer in a wall next to a slum and watched what happened. Within days, the slum children had taught themselves how to surf the net, and download games and music. The experiment, called 'The Hole in the Wall', is now being replicated in other Indian cities.

Paragraph 3
When a person says 'sums up' for 'thumbs up', we dismiss it as a slip of the tongue. Linguists take such errors seriously because they show how the human mind works. For example, when 'speech production' comes out as 'preach seduction', it shows that the speaker already plans to use the word 'production'. So, this everyday phenomenon is an important source of information for linguists.

2. Delete the following sentence: *The Internet was originally set up in the 1970s for defence purposes.*
3. However, the use of technology varies widely across departments.
4. Many people are surprised to learn that dinosaurs could be both very large and fairly tiny.
5. (a) It is clear that most college graduates today (T) are familiar with technology (C).
   (b) Through the ages, linguists (T) have studied how languages work (C).
   (c) How history is interpreted (T) depends on the time and the ideology of the historian (C).
   (d) Our habits and feelings (T) often seem to hinder our writing (C).
6. The concluding sentence should provide a suggestion. Here are some possible concluding sentences.
   - See the movie if you must.
   - Strictly for twits.
   - Watch it for the scenery.

CHAPTER

5

Simple Paragraph Types

INTRODUCTION

So far we have looked at the structure of a generic paragraph. But often paragraphs (and even texts) have an additional layer that is familiar to readers. Readers begin reading a paragraph and say, 'Oh, here's the procedure' or 'Here come the causes and results'. There are six clear text types that are familiar to readers and that you can use when writing paragraphs (and texts). These six text types are listed below, along with the chapter in which it is covered.

1. Enumeration or listing (Chapter 5)
2. Exemplification or giving examples (Chapter 5)
3. Sequence of events or activities (Chapter 6)
4. Comparison of items (Chapter 6)
5. Cause-Effect relationships (Chapter 7)
6. Description of visuals (Chapter 7)

A long text uses a combination of these text types, moving from one to another seamlessly. However, scrutinising each text type separately helps you recognise how they are structured and how to write such texts.

A text type is also signalled by certain words that show the connection between sentences. These words are called transition signals or connectives. Here are some examples.

> **Enumeration**: There are several reasons why women are paid less than men for equal work. *First,....*
>
> **Cause and effect**: Women receive lower wages primarily *because* men are in charge of setting salaries.

If you omit these transition signals, the connection between the sentences remains unclear.

> There are several reasons why women are paid less than men for equal work. Men are in charge of setting salaries.

Transition words are not interchangeable because they signal different relationships, and for each relationship you should use the appropriate signalling words. For each text type, we have given a partial list of transition signals along with common pitfalls.

ENUMERATION

The simplest way to provide information is to list it.

> In sentences: She bought apples, spinach and sugar.
>
> In paragraphs: Several factors have led to the problems in schools. First, the lack of funding....

Since this is the loosest form of organisation, there is a danger that the information will turn into a mere list of facts that cannot be easily understood or remembered. Here is an example where several facts have been thrown in.

> Employees will be assessed on *four* parameters: level of responsibilities, independence, accountability, project completion, quality of the project, client satisfaction, client feedback.

The paragraph says there are four parameters, but the list contains seven items. If we examine the seven items closely, we see that they fall into four groups: (a) responsibilities, (b) independence and accountability, (c) the project, and (d) client responses. This is what the writer meant to say.

> The employees were assessed on *four* parameters: level of responsibilities, independence and accountability, project completion and quality, and client satisfaction and feedback.

The list becomes clearer if similar items are grouped with the word *and*, and different groups of items are separated by commas.

Criteria for a List

When texts begin with the words and sentences given below, we expect a list of items to follow.

- Two *methods* are commonly used to analyse such data: quantitative and qualitative.
- A paragraph has three *sections*: a topic sentence, supporting details, and a concluding sentence.

As far as possible, we try to organise the list of items. For example, even a laundry list is not arbitrary but is sorted by some criterion as follows.

- Size—large versus small items
- Colour—whites versus coloureds

So, enumeration is a text type in which we use some criterion to sort information before we list it.

Organising a List

When you have a list of points, the simplest way to organise them is by order of importance. Begin with the most important and end with the least important.

Example from your resume

Relevant skills for the position of Project Leader

- Good interpersonal skills (most important skill)
- Excellent technical knowledge (next most important skill)
- Most senior person on the staff (least important skill)

There are other ways to list items. Go to the exercise at the end of this chapter to see some of these methods.

Order of Mention

Suppose you mention two facts or examples and then go on to describe each one. In your description, you should describe them in the order in which you mentioned them. This is because readers set up a framework in their heads that tends to be a hierarchy and not a chain.

Example of a chain

This smartphone is both **small** and **elegant**. It has a sleek **design** and it **fits** in the palm of your hand.

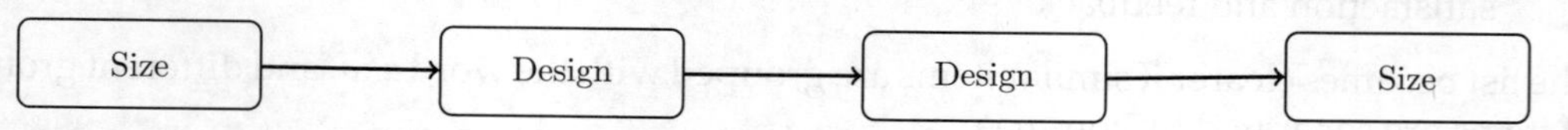

Figure 5.1: Chained list

Example of a hierarchy

This smartphone is both **small** and **elegant**. It is only as **big** as your palm and it has a sleek **design**.

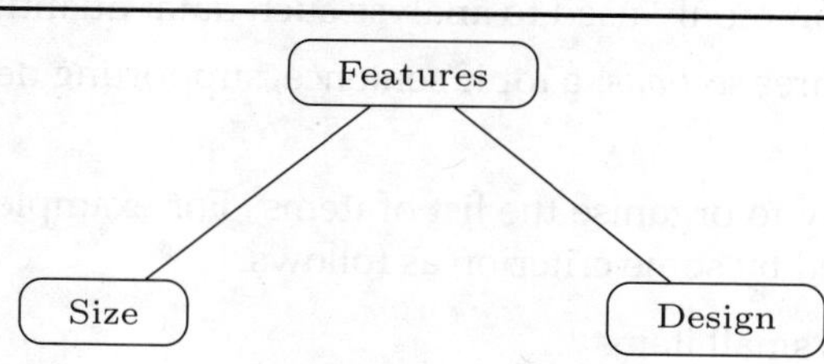

Figure 5.2: Hierarchical list

Transition Signals for Enumeration

In sentences, we sometimes reel off a series of items. Notice that we use *and* before the last item.

The system uses a television screen, an amplifier, *and* five speakers.

But to connect sentences we do not use *and,* because it is considered too informal in writing. Instead, we use signals such as *also, moreover,* or *in addition.*

- The camera is light. *Also,* it is inexpensive.
- The camera is light. *Moreover,* it is inexpensive.
- The camera is light. *In addition,* it is inexpensive.

Transition Signals for Enumeration		
and	further	moreover
too	besides	in addition
again	also	equally important

One transition signal is enough! The sentence below has two transition signals that mean the same—*further* and *also.* Delete one of them.

Further, the administrative procedures are *also* complicated.
Solution: *Further,* the administrative procedures are complicated.

EXEMPLIFICATION

Exemplification, or giving examples, helps readers link abstract ideas to concrete instances. They also support your claims.

The study found that children in primary school had poor number recognition.

What does this mean? An example makes it clear.

For instance, most of the students in Class 2 could not recognise numbers from 0 to 9.

Here are some sentences that give examples.

- Fluent readers use a mix of strategies, such as skimming, scanning, and re-reading. Readers understand what you mean by *strategies.*
- The study found that the infrastructure was poor. For example, the number of classrooms was inadequate.

The example supports your claim.

Transition Signals for Examples		
e.g.,	to illustrate	take the case of
for instance	as an illustration	in another case
for example	to demonstrate	such as

Common Mistakes

Examples are the easiest way to explain your ideas, but be careful when writing. Here are some incorrect ways of giving examples. Can you spot the errors?

1. For example, Toyota, Mitsubishi, and Honda.
2. Many companies, eg, Toyota, use JIT.
3. Many companies, for e.g., use JIT.
4. Many companies, such as Toyota, Mitsubishi, etc. use JIT.

Answers

1. The sentence does not have a verb. We can correct this by adding a verb.
    - For example, Toyota, Mitsubishi, and Honda *use* JIT.
    - Examples *include* Toyota, Mitsubishi, and Honda.
2. Spelling of *e.g.*
   e.g. is spelt incorrectly. Note the full stops between the letters, followed by a comma.
    - Many companies, e.g., Toyota, use JIT.

   We avoid using *e.g.* in formal writing. Use it if you are short of space, but otherwise use a complete form such as *for example.*
3. Using *for e.g.*
   e.g. means *for example.* If you write *for e.g.*, you have said *for for example.*
4. Using *etc.* with examples
   This is repetition, because *such as* and *etc.* mean the same. Use only one of these phrases.
    - Many companies, such as Toyota and Mitsubishi, use JIT.
    - Toyota, Mitsubishi, etc. use JIT.

EXERCISES

Q1. The following sentences consist of lists of items. Decide where you would use *and.*

1. Activities like spinning, dyeing, drying can be mechanised.
2. Hydroelectric power is necessary for sectors such as. agriculture, weaving, tourism.
3. To improve social conditions, it is necessary to improve indicators like health conditions, water availability, electricity, sanitation, infrastructure like roads, markets, telecommunications.

Q2. The two items below consist of phrases. Rewrite each one as a complete sentence that lists a series of items. Remember to use the word *and* correctly.

1. Develop: products, technology, the capabilities of the management, the capabilities of the staff.
2. Sectors that are strongly linked: heavy machinery, infrastructure, fast-moving consumer goods, luxury goods, food, housing.

Q3. In the texts below, examine the transition signals. Delete repetitions and join sentences where needed.

1. To handle the rush, the bank hired extra tellers. Moreover, the bank also set up extra ATMs in the city.
2. The study found that the river had been polluted by waste from chemical plants. And these effluents were dangerous to humans and livestock in the neighbourhood.

Q4. How would you organise the list of items in each sentence?

1. This list includes countries such as Germany, China, the Netherlands, the UK, Brazil, the US.
2. Trees on campus should not be cut down. They lend character to the campus and provide a pleasant ambience. Further, it takes years for trees to grow and they cannot be easily replaced. Finally, by cutting down trees we hasten global warming.
3. There are six levels in the Bloom taxonomy:

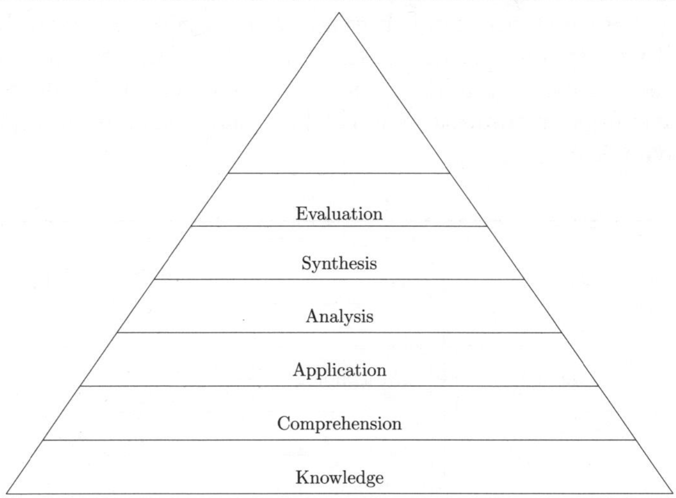

Figure 1: Bloom taxonomy

Q5. The paragraphs below are confusing because the items do not follow the order in which they are listed. What changes would you make?

1. Two factors contribute to the problems in higher education: the problem of quality teachers and the lack of funds. The problem of funds can be addressed by increasing the government's monetary allocations, by making amendments that encourage institutions to invest in order to generate internal revenue, and by offering short-term courses to corporate houses. The problem of quality faculty is more deep-rooted and, therefore, more difficult to solve.
2. In Japan, the industrial sector contributes 29% to GDP and the agricultural sector accounts for a mere 1.6% of the economy. In contrast, the Indian economy contributes 18% and 28% to GDP from the agriculture and industry sectors, respectively.

Q6. Find the errors in the following sentences and correct them.

1. Most of the world's diamonds come from central and southern Africa, but the mineral has also been discovered in countries such as Canada, Russia, Brazil, etc.
2. Global warming is caused by many factors. For example, carbon dioxide emitted from cars, power plants, and buildings.
3. The company produces household tools, such as pliers, scissors, etc.
4. The library has books in the social sciences (e.g. psychology, sociology, etc.) as well as journals, magazines, etc.
5. The state should develop local agricultural industries (e.g., fruits, fruit juices, jams, herbs) and handicrafts (e.g. shawls, woolens, hosiery etc.).

Q7. Read the following text and use the information to complete the boxes in the diagram that follows.

> Linguistics is the study of language and linguists study language at different levels. In phonology, they are concerned with the sounds of a language. For instance, English makes a distinction between the sounds *b* and *v*. In morphology, they study how words are formed; in English, plurals are formed by adding the *-s* morpheme. At the next level, they examine syntax or grammar, such as how active sentences can be changed to passive voice.

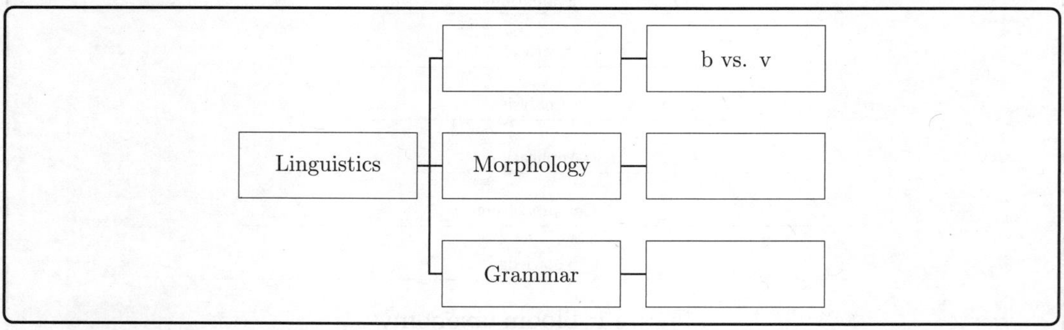

Q8. The text below does not provide any examples, making it abstract and difficult to follow. Add examples for each category so that you can relate the text to your own experience.

Films may look different from one another but they fall into a few limited types. Comedies are light-hearted with witty dialogues and funny social situations. Horror films are designed to scare you; they may involve ghosts or a terror that is closer to reality. People go to see action films for their stunts, fights, chases and narrow escapes; the plot moves at a rapid pace, allowing no time for thought. Sci-fi films tend to be futuristic; they depict an alien universe, complete with strange inhabitants and advanced technology. The gangster film has become increasingly popular; these portray the underworld and the life of people who live outside the law. War movies either glorify the sacrifice of soldiers or present the horrors of war. Films can have elements of many genres but if you look at a film review, you will find that a film is tagged with a certain category.

ANSWERS

1. 1. Activities like spinning, dyeing *and* drying can be mechanised.
   2. Hydroelectric power is necessary for sectors such as agriculture, weaving *and* tourism.
   3. To improve social conditions, it is necessary to improve indicators like health conditions, water availability, electricity *and* sanitation, *and* infrastructure like roads, markets *and* telecommunications.
2. 1. We need to develop our products, technology and the capabilities of the management and the staff in a consistent manner.
   2. Sectors that are strongly linked are heavy machinery and infrastructure, fast-moving consumer goods and luxury goods, and food and housing.
3. 1. To handle the rush, the bank hired extra tellers. Moreover, the bank set up extra ATMs in the city.
   2. The study found that the river had been polluted by waste from chemical plants, and these effluents were dangerous to humans and livestock in the neighbourhood.
4. 1. You can organise this list alphabetically.
      This list includes countries such as Brazil, China, Germany, the Netherlands, the UK, and the US.
   2. Organise the points by their importance.
      Trees on campus should not be cut down. By cutting down trees we hasten global warming. Further, it takes years for trees to grow and they cannot be easily replaced. Finally, they lend character to the campus and provide a pleasant ambience.
   3. Organise this list from the lowest to the highest.
      There are six levels in the Bloom taxonomy: knowledge, comprehension, application, analysis, synthesis, and evaluation.
5. 1. Two factors contribute to the problems in higher education: *the lack of funds and the problem of quality teachers*. The problem of funds can be addressed by increasing the government's monetary allocations, by making amendments that

encourage institutions to invest in order to generate internal revenue, and by offering short-term courses to corporate houses. The problem of quality faculty is more deep-rooted and, therefore, more difficult to solve.

2. In Japan, the industrial sector contributes 29% to GDP and the agricultural sector accounts for a mere 1.6% of the economy. In contrast, the Indian economy contributes *28% and 18% to GDP from the industry and agriculture sectors*, respectively.

6. 1. Most of the world's diamonds come from central and southern Africa, but the mineral has also been discovered in countries such as Canada, Russia *and* Brazil.
   2. Global warming is caused by many factors, *such as* carbon dioxide emitted from cars, power plants, and buildings.
   3. The company produces household tools, such as pliers *and* scissors.
   4. The library has books in the social sciences (*e.g.*, psychology and sociology) as well as journals, magazines, etc.
   5. The state should develop local agricultural industries (e.g., fruits, fruit juices, jams *and* herbs) and handicrafts (e.g., shawls, woollens *and* hosiery).

7.

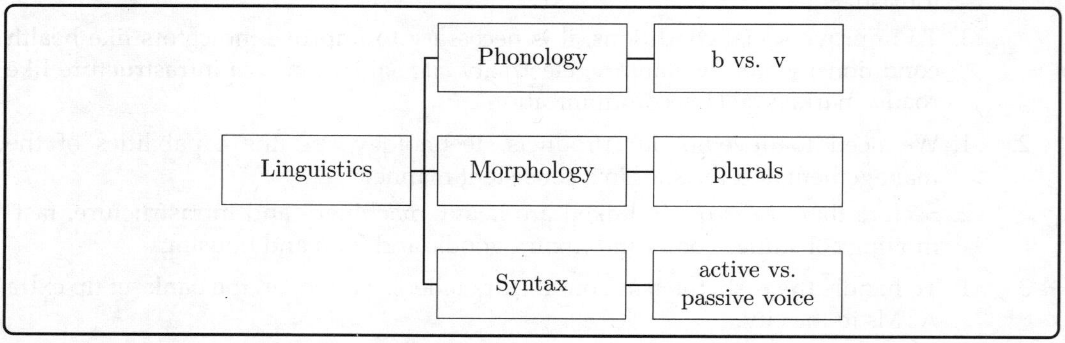

8. Here is a possible answer.

Films may look different from one another but they fall into a few limited types. Comedies, such as *3 Idiots*, are light-hearted with witty dialogues and funny social situations. Horror films are designed to scare you; for instance, they may involve ghosts or a terror that is closer to reality. People go to see action films for their stunts, fights, chases and narrow escapes; in *Dhoom 3*, for example, the plot moves at a rapid pace, allowing no time for thought. Sci-fi films tend to be futuristic; they depict an alien universe, complete with strange inhabitants and advanced technology; *Love Story 2050* is such a movie. The gangster film has become increasingly popular; these portray the underworld and the life of people who live outside the law; we see this in various versions of *Don*. War movies either glorify the sacrifice of soldiers as in *Border* or present the horrors of war, as in *Letters from Iwo Jima*. Films can have elements of many genres but if you look at a film review, you will find that a film is tagged with a certain category.

CHAPTER

6 More Complex Paragraphs

INTRODUCTION

Listing items and giving examples are two simple ways to organise information in paragraphs. But there can be more complex relationships between ideas. In this chapter we will look at two ways to organise paragraphs that describe the following:

1. **A sequence**. We know this from stories and our history textbooks. It comes up again at the university in lab reports, case studies, and your resume.
2. **A comparison of items**. You may be asked to evaluate two theories or two solutions. For this, you have to find the points on which they are similar, but also identify their differences.

Although students use these two text types in school, they find it difficult to read (and write) such texts at the university, perhaps because they cannot see the link. This chapter covers the basic logic of these text types, and the steps to follow. The exercises use non-academic texts so that you can check whether or not you understand the logic.

SEQUENCE

Several texts describe a sequence of events. Think of a cookery book, a computer manual, a history text, or your bio-data. In all of them, the events are listed in an order that is based on the passage of time. In effect, it is a timeline.

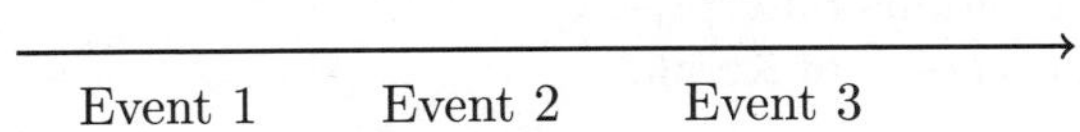

Figure 6.1: Timeline

Texts that are structured based on a sequence of events fall into two types: a chronology of events and a process/procedure.

Chronology

This is a description of events arranged by the time when they occurred. Here are some areas where we find such texts.

Narratives

Once upon a time, there was a beautiful princess. Once day she saw a frog in the forest. She went up to the frog and kissed it. She turned into a frog. They lived happily ever after.

Historical events

Financial liberalisation affected the US and UK financial systems in the 1970s, most other advanced countries in the 1980s, and the less developed economies only in the past decade.

Case studies

Global Ltd. faced a crisis in 2009. After it was set up in 1970, it slowly grew into the country's leading manufacturer of cathode ray tubes. By the 1990s, it was also supplying CRTs to a company in Japan. It faced its first crisis when the Japanese company opted out of the TV hardware business in 2007 and Global Ltd. had to look for an alternative market. In 2008, it identified a company in China, but....

Curriculum vitae or bio-data

This is usually in reverse chronological order, with the most recent event listed first.

2016 Project Leader, Wunderkind Solutions
2014 Team member, Prodigious Enterprises
2012 B.A. in History, University of Kerala

Transition Signals for Time		
earlier	later	now
previously	soon	at this time
before this	then	at this point
after	following this	

Process/Procedure

Processes are common in the sciences.

Example
The water cycle describes how water circulates between the land and the atmosphere. Heat from the sun causes water from rivers and oceans to turn into vapour that rises. When the vapour meets the cooler air in the atmosphere, it condenses into droplets in clouds. If the clouds meet cold air, the water condenses and falls to earth as rain.

A procedure describes a sequence of steps to accomplish a task. This is found in manuals, instruction booklets, cookery books, etc.

Examples

1. How to change your password in Gmail.

   Step 1: Sign in to Gmail.
   Step 2: Click Settings at the top of any Gmail page, and open the Accounts and Import tab.
   Step 3: Click Google Account settings.
   Step 4: In the new window, click Change password under the Personal information option.
   Step 5: Enter your current password and then your new password.

2. Procedures are common in disciplines such as physics, chemistry and biology where manufacturing or laboratory procedures are described. In the social sciences, this text type is used to describe data collection and analysis.
   - The questionnaire was administered to 36 participants. Their responses were coded into four categories....
   - To reduce the number of variables, a one-way ANOVA was conducted, using Government textbooks and Commercial textbooks as the two factors.

Unless there is a compelling reason, describe events in the order in which they occur; otherwise you confuse the reader.

Example
After the law was passed, the number of working women increased to 56% by March 2009 and to 47% by March 2008.

This is confusing because the year 2008 comes before 2009. Narrate events in the order in which they occur. It is better to write:

Example
After the law was passed, the number of working women increased to 47% by March 2008 and to 56% by March 2009.

Transition Signals for Sequence			
first	previously	now	then
second	before this	at this time	soon
third	also	at this point	after
next	simultaneously	concurrently	following this

Comparison of Items

Two people are discussing where to go for a holiday.

> Dev: Delhi's an oven. Let's go where the weather is cooler.
> Preeti: How about Shimla?
> Dev: Manali is better. It's as cold but there are fewer tourists and more scenic spots.

When we compare two items, we need:

- At least two objects to compare. Here, these are Shimla and Manali.
- Some common features. Here, it is the cold weather.
- Some features on which they differ. Here, it is the number of tourists and the number of scenic spots.

The figure below compares two items—A and B. They are similar on some points but differ on others.

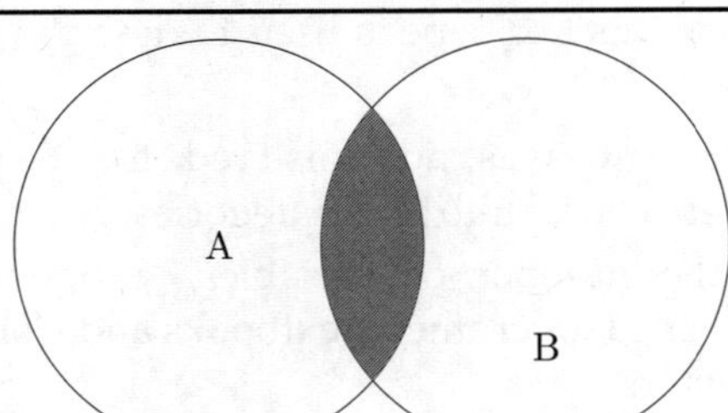

Figure 6.2: Comparing items

This is a very common question in examinations where you are asked to compare and evaluate two or more items. You could be asked to compare two economic trends, three environmental scenarios, four poets, or five techniques.

Steps in Comparing Items

The first step is to draw a table that clearly shows the similarities and differences between the items. We will use a simple example and compare turtles and tortoises on six features.

	Tortoise	Turtle	Comparison
Location	Africa and Asia	Africa and America	X
Species	reptile, amphibious	reptile, amphibious	✓
Habitat	land	water	X
Diet	herbivores	herbivores and carnivores	X
Lifespan	100 years	30 years	X
Shell	heavy, dome-shaped	light and flat	X

Once you have the information, you can easily pick up each point and elaborate on it. Here, two types of organisation are possible: block organisation or feature-by-feature organisation.

Block organisation

In block organisation you first describe how the two items are similar and follow this with a paragraph on their differences.

Similarities	**Both** tortoises and turtles are reptiles that are amphibious, that is, they can live on both land and water. Their bodies are protected by a hard shell.
Differences	Although people confuse the two species, there are several important **differences** between tortoises and turtles. They are found in **different** parts of the world; Africa is home to both species, but tortoises are found in Asia, **whereas** turtles are found in America.

Feature-by-feature organisation

You can also compare the two items on each feature.

Topic sentence	People confuse tortoises and turtles because they are so similar, but there are also important differences between the two species.
Location	In terms of their **geographical distribution**, both species are found in Africa but, whereas tortoises are mainly found in Asia, turtles are more common in America.
Species and habitat	Both tortoises and turtles are **reptiles** that can live on both land and water; however, tortoises are mainly found on land, whereas turtles prefer water.
Shell	This preference of habitat is reflected in their **physical characteristics**; tortoises have heavy dome-shaped **shells** whereas a turtle's **shell** is flat and light, which is suitable for swimming...

Transition Signals

Did you notice the words used to signal comparison and contrast in the text above? Here are more transition signals.

Transition Signals for Comparison		
Comparison	**Contrast**	
similarly	but	however
in the same way	whereas	yet
	but	nevertheless
	although	on the other hand

Common problems

On the contrary is often confused with *in contrast.* This is how the two phrases work.

1. I'm not tired. On the contrary, I'm ready for a long hike!

   On the contrary is used to contradict a viewpoint.

2. I'm not tired at all. In contrast, the rest of the team looks exhausted.

   In contrast is used to compare two items.

EXERCISES

Q1. In each paragraph, the sentences are jumbled. Put them in the correct order.

1. **Paragraph 1**
   (a) Books became cheaper and more easily available.
   (b) Few people could afford books, and so most people could not read or write.
   (c) Soon people learned to read and literacy spread among the population.
   (d) However, all this changed around 1455 when Gutenberg invented a printing press with moveable type.
   (e) This allowed multiple copies of a book to be printed rapidly.
   (f) Early books were written by hand, which made them very expensive.
2. **Paragraph 2**
   (a) The dry beans are soaked in water overnight and then ground with some water.
   (b) When it cools, the mixture is filtered to remove the fibres and the liquid is drunk as soy milk.
   (c) Soy milk is made from whole soybeans.
   (d) The mixture is then boiled for about 15 minutes.
3. **Paragraph 3**
   (a) Burton kept detailed records of his journeys.

(b) Richard Francis Burton was a British explorer who came to India in 1842.
(c) Using his facility with languages, he disguised himself as an Indian and worked as a spy for the British.
(d) Some of these were published, but most were burnt by his widow after his death in 1890.
(e) While he was posted in India, he learned numerous languages including Hindi, Gujarati, Punjabi, and Persian.
(f) In 1857-58, together with John Speke, he went in search of the source of the River Nile in Africa and was the first European to reach Lake Tanganyika.
(g) He then made a pilgrimage to Mecca, disguised as an Arab.

Q2. These short texts describe a sequence of events or steps. Read the passages and answer the questions.

Text 1
Brinda takes her dog for a walk every evening. After she puts the dog on a leash, they start out. They head for the market but on the way they stop at the neighbour's house. They return after buying vegetables for dinner. When they reach home, Brinda gives the dog two biscuits.

1. Brinda puts the dog on a leash...
   (a) after they start the walk
   (b) before they start the walk
   (c) during the walk
2. Brinda and the dog stop at the neighbour's house........they reach the market.
   (a) before
   (b) after
   (c) when
3. The dog gets biscuits.........they reach home.
   (a) before
   (b) after
   (c) while
4. Brinda buys vegetables.......visiting the neighbour.
   (a) before
   (b) after
   (c) while

Text 2
Every office needs a fire drill in case there is a fire in the office. Before the drill, a map should be drawn giving the escape routes. Warning signs should also be put up around the office. Then equipment, such as fire extinguishers, should be bought and placed around the office. Next, the office staff should be called for a meeting and only then should the fire drill be held.

1. The meeting should be held........the fire drill
   (a) before
   (b) after
   (c) during
2. Fire extinguishers should be bought.........the meeting.
   (a) before
   (b) after
   (c) during
3. A map showing the escape routes should be made........the meeting.
   (a) after
   (b) at the same time as
   (c) before

Text 3

The class needed to raise money for charity. First, the students held a meeting to discuss ideas and decided on a used book sale. Next, they asked their classmates to donate their used books, which they stored in the classroom. The following week, they sold the books.

1. The students decided on a used book sale........the meeting.
   (a) after
   (b) during
   (c) before
2. They asked their classmates to donate books........the meeting.
   (a) before
   (b) after
   (c) during
3. The books were stored.......they were donated.
   (a) before
   (b) when
   (c) while

Text 4

Before the floods, Maidangarh was a quiet village where people earned a living as farmers and potters. The floods changed all that. The floods brought mud that covered the fields and surrounding land. At first, the farmers were dismayed, but they soon realised that the mud had made the soil richer. Now, the farmers can grow twice as much food. The potters were not so lucky, because the new soil was not suitable for making pots.

1. The farmers grew fewer crops.........the floods.
   (a) before
   (b) after
   (c) during

2. The potters made more pots.........the floods.

   (a) before
   (b) after
   (c) during

Q3. These short texts compare two items. Read the passages and answer the questions.

Text 1
Cars and bicycles are types of transport that people use them to get around. Both cars and bicycles have wheels. But they are also different. Cars have four wheels and an engine. Bicycles have only two wheels and no engine; the rider has to use his feet to make the cycle move.

1. Cars and bicycles are the same in:

   (a) one way
   (b) two ways
   (c) three ways

2. Cars and bicycles are different in:

   (a) one way
   (b) two ways
   (c) three ways

Text 2
Both spinach and carrots are vegetables. They are very nutritious. We can eat them either cooked or uncooked. Spinach is green and leafy, while carrots are red and have long roots.

1. Spinach and carrots are the same in:

   (a) one way
   (b) two ways
   (c) three ways

2. Spinach and carrots are different in:

   (a) one way
   (b) two ways
   (c) three ways

Text 3
My sister and I are going on holiday but we cannot decide where to go. I like the mountains, while she prefers the sea. Both places are nice but they are different. In the mountains, the weather is cold and we can go for long walks. But at the seaside, the weather is warm and we can swim.

1. The mountains and the seaside are the same in:

   (a) one way
   (b) two ways
   (c) three ways

2. The mountains and the seaside are different in:
   (a) one way
   (b) two ways
   (c) three ways

Text 4

The new flat in Pune was as comfortable as their house in the village, but it was also very different. Their old house was made of wood, but the flat was brick and concrete. The old house had a small garden, but this flat on the third floor was bare of greenery. In their old home, they had used lamps, but the flat had electric lights. How they missed their old home!

1. The Pune flat and the village house were the same in:
   (a) one way
   (b) two ways
   (c) three ways
2. The Pune flat and the village house were different in:
   (a) one way
   (b) two ways
   (c) three ways

Q4. What are the similarities and differences between speech and writing? The information is given in the table below. Write a text using this information and add any points you can think of.

Feature	**Speech**	**Writing**
Learning	All humans learn to speak at least one language	Not everyone learns to write. Requires a teacher.
Permanence	transient, vanishes	permanent
Purpose	for social communication	to record facts
Audience	listener is present	reader is absent
Planning	little time is available	can be revised several times
Emphasis	tone and volume are used	typeface, capital letters and punctuation marks are used
Errors	listeners do not notice mistakes in grammar and pronunciation	readers notice language errors
Revision	speaker can adjust message based on listener's cues	cannot be changed once it is submitted

Q5. Your friend wants to buy a new smartphone and has asked for your advice. Find information on two models and prepare a short write-up for your friend. It should include a table of specifications and end with a recommendation.

ANSWERS

1. **Paragraph 1**
   Early books were written by hand, which made them very expensive. Few people could afford books, and so most people could not read or write. However, all this changed around 1455 when Gutenberg invented a printing press with moveable type. This allowed multiple copies of a book to be printed rapidly. Books became cheaper and more easily available. Soon people learned to read and literacy spread among the population.

   Paragraph 2
   Soymilk is made from whole soybeans. The dry beans are soaked in water overnight and then ground with some water. The mixture is then boiled for about 15 minutes. When it cools, the mixture is filtered to remove the fibres and the liquid is drunk as soymilk.

   Paragraph 3
   Richard Francis Burton was a British explorer who came to India in 1842. While he was posted in India, he learned numerous languages including Hindi, Gujarati, Punjabi, and Persian. Using his facility with languages, he disguised himself as an Indian and worked as a spy for the British. He then made a pilgrimage to Mecca, disguised as a Arab. In 1857–58, together with John Speke, he went in search of the source of the River Nile in Africa and was the first European to reach Lake Tanganyika. Burton kept detailed records of his journeys. Some of these were published, but most were burnt by his widow after his death in 1890.

2. Text 1: 1. b, 2. a, 3. b, 4. b
   Text 2: 1. a, 2. a, 3. c
   Text 3: 1. b, 2. b, 3. b
   Text 4: 1. a, 2. a

3. Text 1: 1. b, 2. b
   Text 2: 1. c, 2. b
   Text 3: 1. a, 2. b
   Text 4: 1. a, 2. c

CHAPTER 7

Describing Cause-Effect and Visuals

INTRODUCTION

This chapter wraps up the discussion on text types by covering two types of paragraphs:

1. **Cause-effect**. These paragraphs or texts describe the causes or results of an event or action. This text type appears to be the most difficult one for readers to understand, often because the connection between the cause and the effect is not clearly stated.
2. **Description of visuals**. Many academic texts contain visuals such as graphs, images, and diagrams. If you use visuals, you need to describe them.

Cause-Effect Relationships

The two sentences below express a cause-effect relationship. In the first sentence, the cause is mentioned first, but in the second sentence the effect comes first.

a. The earthquake *caused* a tsunami.

Cause → Effect

b. The tsunami *was caused* by an earthquake.

Effect ← Cause

Next, look at a sentence that does *not* show a cause-effect relationship.

India spends little on education *and* literacy levels are low.

The writer states two facts, but does not say that one causes the other. If there is a causal link, the sentence would be:

India spends little on education, *so* literacy levels are low.

Cause-effect relationships lie at the heart of all disciplines. Every discipline tries to identify the reasons for a phenomenon or the effects of an action. You can see this in the table below that tries to identify the causes and consequences of rural migration.

Causes	Phenomenon	Consequences
Natural disasters (floods, droughts)	Rural migration	Food insecurity for the country
Poor living conditions (healthcare, education)		Overcrowding in cities

A cause-effect relationship is often complex, involving a chain of causes and consequences.

> **Example**
> When farmers migrate to the city, agricultural activity is reduced, which leads to food insecurity for the country.
>
> The chain looks like the following:
> Rural migration → drop in farming activities → food insecurity for the country

Causal relationships are at the core of any job. In industry, there are constant efforts to identify problems and improve processes. Often, a team uses a fishbone diagram to identify all possible causes.

It is also common in trouble shooting or problem solving.

My computer is running very slow.

1. Why? There is a virus. Run a virus scan. No virus found.
2. Why? The disk is fragmented. Run Disk Fragmentation. No problem here.
3. Why? A process is running in the background. Check all running processes. Oh! I thought I had shut down SPSS, but it is still running and eating up memory.

Transition Signals

Although cause-effect relationships are important in academic writing, they are often not explicitly signalled but are implied through verbs.

X *allows* Y

X *enables* Y

X *influences* Y

X *generates* Y

X *gives rise to* Y

Many writers use a simple connective such as *and*, leaving it to the reader to figure out the causal relationship.

Transition Signals for Cause-Effect Relationships

Cause	Effect
as	hence
due to	thereby
because	thus
since	as a result
the reason	consequently
	therefore

Common problems

Since and *as* are commonly used to suggest cause but have other meanings.

a. He was exhausted *since* he had been working *since* morning.

b. He was exhausted *as* he had worked for *as* long *as* 10 hours.

In something as important as a cause-effect relationship, if you use *as* to signal a cause, the relationship may not be understood. In sentence 1 below, *as* means *that are,* but in sentence 2 *as* is used to mean *because.*

1. The model includes other variables *as* special or limiting cases.
2. The model does not include environmental factors *as* there is no data on these factors.

Use *because* when you mean *because.*

Describing Visuals

Many texts do not merely use words, but, for various reasons, they include visuals, such as images, line drawings or graphs. These are especially common in the sciences, where texts include illustrations of apparatus or spectrograms, or flowcharts. These visuals help the reader by showing unfamiliar material (in an image), depicting abstract concepts (in a line drawing), or collapsing information in a visual form (graphs).

The problem is that readers may not understand your visual. All the information is presented simultaneously instead of piece by piece, which can be bewildering to readers. Further, some visuals, such as photographs, are packed with information, some of which may not be relevant to your point. Which part of the picture should the reader look at? You need to direct the reader's attention to the salient parts of the visual. A line drawing is sparser than an image; in fact, it can be so sparse that the reader cannot understand what it means, so you have to explain what the drawing means.

Here we cover two aspects: spatial order and describing visuals in a research paper.

Spatial Order

Spatial order presents the details of a visual (or scene) in terms of their location in a space. For example, we could describe a visual from left to right or from the centre to outwards. However, there are a few complications.

Left to right

Figure 7.1 shows what a 3-and-a-half-year-old child produced when she was learning to write. After she learnt the letters of the English alphabet, she tried to arrange them in a sequence and came up with Boustrophedon writing—left to right, then right to left. Incidentally, this form was used in some ancient scripts before they settled down to using either left to right as in English, or right to left as in Hebrew or Urdu, much like the 3-and-a-half-year-old child did. Adults become used to one reading pattern and apply it to visuals. So, English readers scan a visual from left to right, but it is the reverse with Urdu readers. This fact is usually ignored in an English-centric world, and I will do the same in the discussion below.

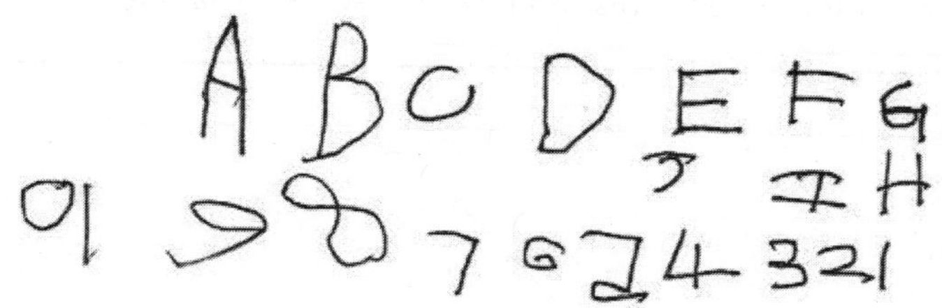

Figure 7.1: Boustrophedon writing produced by a 3-and-a-half-year-old child

Practical work
Either find an image of a fish or draw a simple diagram. Then, try to describe the picture. You will probably find the following:

1. The fish is shown with the front end on the left.
2. Your description begins from the front of the fish (at the left) and moves to the back (at the right).

Centre to the periphery

Sometimes, we use a spatial order that begins from the centre and then moves outwards.

Example
The Earth is spherical. The Equator runs around the centre, with the....

Global, followed by details

A third method of describing an object is to first give a global picture and then provide details. We use this method when we describe a building.

> The shopping mall has four floors. Groceries are located on the first floor, men's wear on the second, women's wear on the third, and a food court right on top.

Line Drawings and Photographs

The figures below form part of two texts. How do we describe them?

Line drawing

Figure 7.2 presents a model of education in which the three principal components—curriculum, teaching, and testing—do not occur in isolation, but have equal importance and are interrelated. This can be depicted as a triangle.

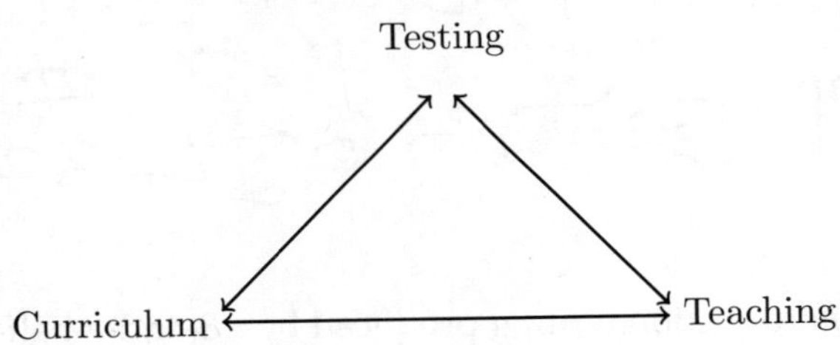

Figure 7.2: Model of education

This description goes from the details to the global picture.

Images

Images contain more information than is required. Your explanation should extract the relevant information and then present it in an order that readers can follow.

For the image below, the description follows the logic below.

1. Prominent items first.
2. Items in the centre first; then, move to objects further from the centre.
3. From left to right, because we are used to scanning in that direction.

Description of Japanese manual typewriter
Written Japanese uses hundreds of individual characters and hence the typewriter was re-designed to incorporate these characters. Figure 7.3 shows the principal components of a Japanese typewriter. The tray in the centre contains hundreds of individual characters. The typist uses the lever on the left to move this tray around and the lever on the right to pick up a character. By depressing the right lever, the typist types the character on the roll of paper that can be seen above the tray.

Figure 7.3: Japanese manual typewriter

Notice that several components of the photo have been omitted—the spool on the left, the picking device in the centre, etc.—because they have peripheral functions.

Some More Transition Signals		
above	behind	in front
alongside	beneath	near
on top of	upon	below
down	under	next to
to the left/right		

Figures

Numbers are difficult to interpret, so we often present them in a visual form. We see this in newspapers that show the numbers in the form of a pie chart (Figure 7.4) or a bar graph (Figure 7.5). Pie charts are easy to understand, but notice the problem—you can only report one set of numbers in a pie chart (boys versus girls), whereas a bar graph will also allow you to compare their choice on football versus karate.

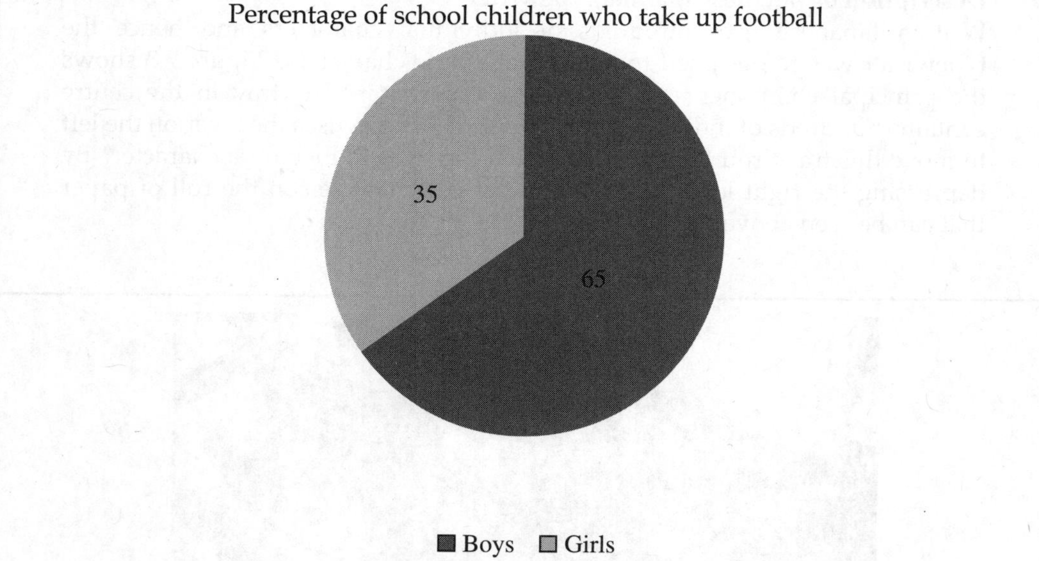

Figure 7.4: Piechart

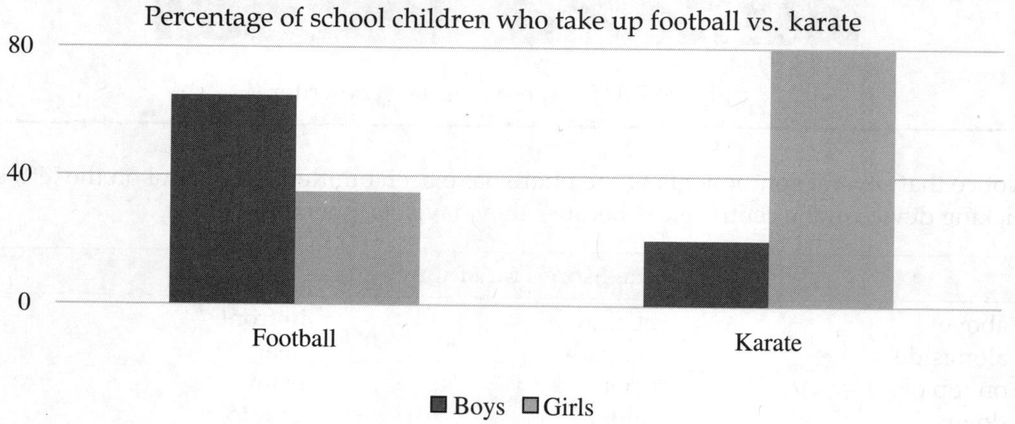

Figure 7.5: Bar graph

How does one describe such figures? In examinations that test your academic reading and writing skills, you may be given a figure (with a background note) and asked to write 150 words that describe it. Since these are academic tasks, the figures are more complex than what a newspaper reader can understand. The figure may show a trend over time, for which we use a line graph.

Figure 7.6: Line graph

The graph compares the after-school activities of boys and girls between 2012 and 2017. Overall, the graph shows that boys begin with higher participation than girls in 2012 (30% vs. 20%, respectively), but by 2017 their participation is lower ((10% vs. 50%, respectively). The change is not steady and there are fluctuations during this period. For boys, after-school activities peak in 2013 (40%) but then decline to zero in 2015; participation picks up, but only to 10% in both 2015 and 2016. For girls, there is a steady decline from 20% in 2012 to 5% in 2016; this is followed by a sharp increase to 50% in 2017.	Direct attention to the visual. If possible, give a global picture. Explain individual trends. Give important numbers.
A comparison of the trends for boys and girls shows a shift around 2006–07. Participation by both boys and girls picked up, but the increase was larger for girls. While boys? participation rose by 10%, for girls it increased by as much as 40%.	Interpret the trends. Do not go beyond the data or speculate.

There are four important points to remember.

1. Use a phrase to direct attention to the visual. *The chart shows....*
2. Draw attention *only* to the important features of the visual. Do not start from the left and describe every number all the way to the right end of the graphic. Readers can find the details if they want; you need to focus on the main numbers or trends.

3. Comment on the visual and what it shows. The visual has been used to make a point. It contains extra information, so draw attention to the point you are making. Otherwise, the reader will ask, 'So what?'
4. Do *not* make claims that are not supported by the data. You might be tempted to say 'Girls today are actively involved in after-school activities, which may be a new trend.' This is not supported by the data; in fact, it may be the reverse but you do not know. Without hard evidence, you cannot make claims or speculate about possible links and causes.

To describe trends, we use specific verbs. These are shown below.

Words used to Describe Trends

Symbol	**Meaning**
↗	increase, rise, climb
↗	soar, shoot up
↘	decline, decrease, drop, fall, slide
↘	crash, collapse, plunge
→	remain steady, stabilise
⇝	fluctuate

EXERCISES

Q1. Which of the following topics require a cause-effect essay?

(a) The role of museums today
(b) The effects of greenhouse gases
(c) How to choose the best broadband provider
(d) Why people exercise
(e) The increasing use of online shopping

Q2. Below is a list of topics for an essay. Decide which topics require causes, which ones want consequences, and those that require both causes and results.

(a) Why texting has become popular
(b) The causes and effects of air pollution
(c) Why I chose to study this subject
(d) Why people still read newspapers
(e) The impact of computers in our everyday lives
(f) The downside of smartphones
(g) The impact of bottled water on the environment

Q3. Fill in the blanks with *since* or *so*.

(a) Farmers need land, ...they cut down forests.
(b) Rainforests are cleared.....there is a demand for timber.

(c) Tree roots anchor the soil, ...deforestation leads to soil erosion that can result in flooding and landslides.

(d) .... 70% of the world's plants and animals live in forests, deforestation may lead to the extinction of species.

Q4. These short texts describe cause and effect relationships. Read the passages and answer the questions.

Text 1

If you go to a wildlife sanctuary, you will be lucky to see a wild elephant. The number of elephants in the wild has been decreasing. The main reason is that elephants are killed for their tusks. But another reason is that we have cut down the forests where these animals live, and so they have less food and space to roam. The species will die out if we do not act soon.

1. Why is the number of elephants decreasing?
   (a) for one reason
   (b) for two reasons
   (c) for three reasons
2. Elephants have less food:
   (a) because we have cut down the forests.
   (b) so we have cut down the forests.
   (c) because they have less space to roam.

Text 2

We went for a bicycle race today, but Seema did not make it to the end. That's because she's not fit. She eats junk food like chips and cakes. She also hates to exercise; getting up in the morning is her main exercise for the day. And then she reads storybooks till late at night, so she does not get enough sleep. No wonder Seema's health is poor.

1. Why is Seema's health poor?
   (a) for one reason
   (b) for two reasons
   (c) for three reasons
2. Seema does not get enough sleep:
   (a) because she reads late at night.
   (b) so she reads late at night.
   (c) because she is not sleepy.

Text 3

Life in Delhi is very difficult. The climate is extreme—too hot in summer and too cold in winter. So people use air conditioners in summer and heaters in winter. But since there is not enough electricity, frequently there are power cuts. Yet people still love Delhi and refuse to move out.

1. It is difficult to live in Delhi:
   (a) for one reason

(b) for two reasons
(c) for three reasons

2. There are power cuts:

(a) because there is not enough electricity.
(b) so there is not enough electricity.
(c) since people use air conditioners.

Text 4

Global warming has become a major problem. The cars we drive release gases into the air that make it warmer. Forest fires to clear the land also lead to global warming. The effects are alarming. The climate has changed and the weather is hotter. The level of the ocean is rising, because the ice is melting. Countries are now thinking of ways to stop global warming.

1. Global warming is due to:

(a) one reason
(b) two reasons
(c) three reasons

2. The sea level is rising:

(a) because the ice is melting.
(b) so the ice is melting.
(c) so the weather is hotter.

Q5. Which strategy would you use to describe the following?

(a) An amoeba
(b) A bicycle
(c) A map showing the physical features of South India

Q6. The figure shows the data collected from one school on after-school activities. It reports the numbers for 200 students, 100 boys and 100 girls. Write 150 words describing the information shown in the figure.

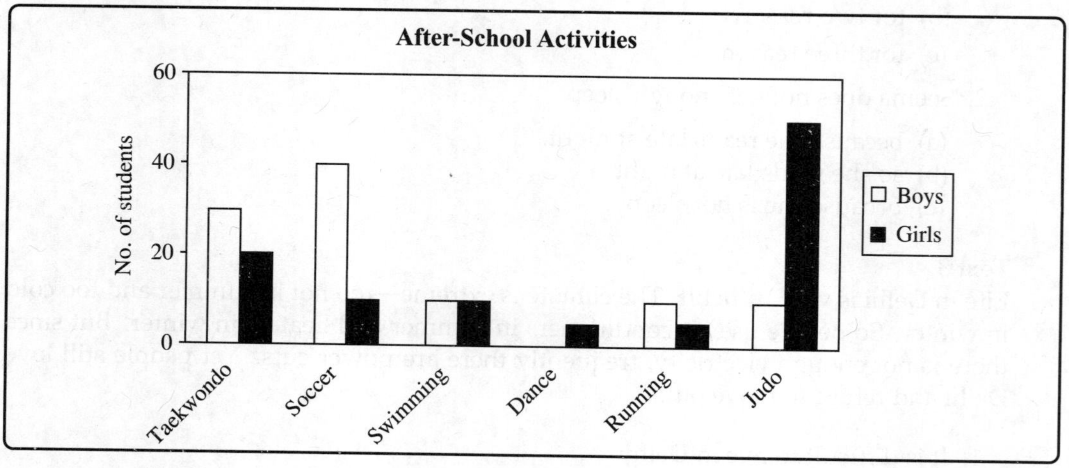

ANSWERS

1. • The effects of greenhouse gases
   • Why people exercise

2. Essays on causes

   • Why texting has become popular
   • Why I chose to study this subject
   • Why people still read newspapers

   Essays on effects

   • The impact of computers in our everyday lives
   • The downside of smartphones
   • The impact of bottled water on the environment

   Essays on both causes and effects

   • The causes and effects of air pollution

3. 1. Farmers need land, *so* they cut down forests.
   2. Rainforests are cleared *since* there is a demand for timber.
   3. Tree roots anchor the soil, *so* deforestation leads to soil erosion that can result in flooding and landslides.
   4. *Since* 70% of the world's plants and animals live in forests, deforestation may lead to the extinction of species.

4. Text 1: 1. b, 2. a
   Text 2: 1. c, 2. a
   Text 3: 1. b, 2. a
   Text 4: 1. b, 2. a

5. a. An amoeba. Centre outwards.
   b. A bicycle. Left to right
   c. A map showing the physical features of South India. Global to details.

6. *The bar chart* presents information on the after-school activities of boys and girls (n=200).

   The chart shows that all students were involved in some form of after-school activity, but there were differences between the activities selected by boys versus girls, as well as between contact sports and non-contact activities.

   Among girls, judo is the single most popular activity (50), while the other half is distributed between Taekwondo (20), soccer and swimming (10 each) and dance and running (5 each). For boys, soccer (40) and Taekwondo (30) are almost equally popular. For running, swimming and judo, there are 10 boys in each activity. Dance seems to be unpopular, with no boys taking up this activity.

Contact sports (Taekwondo, soccer, and judo) are more popular than non-contact activities (swimming running, and dance). Among the contact sports, Taekwondo and soccer are more popular with boys, whereas more girls than boys take up judo.

This shows that there is a clear preference for contact sports among both boys and girls.

CHAPTER 8

The Language of Reports and Research Papers

INTRODUCTION

In the previous chapters, we looked at paragraphs, but now we will deal with entire texts. You know that a letter looks different from a story or an advertisement. They are different types of texts, which we call *genres*. They have different formats, audiences and purposes. And so the language in them differs. In the same way, there are differences between newspaper articles, reports and academic papers. In this chapter, we look at the language in some genres and examine the following aspects.

1. Informing versus persuading
2. Purpose and audience
3. Formal versus informal language

Informing versus Persuading

The two letters below are from the same organisation—a bank to the same customer. But they have different purposes. Letter 1 merely provides the customer with necessary information, whereas Letter 2 tries to persuade the customer to do something. Notice the difference in the language they use. The informative text uses formal language that creates a distance between the bank and the customer. In contrast, the persuasive text tries to reduce this distance by using a friendly style; it has short sentences, exclamation marks, and emotive adjectives (*exorbitant, loved*).

Letter 1. Your monthly statement

Dear Customer,

Your BetterBank account e-statement is being sent to you as a pdf document.

To open this file, you need Adobe Acrobat Reader. If you do not have Adobe Acrobat Reader, please visit the following link to download it:
www.adobe.com/products/acrobat/readstep2.html

To view your statement, enter the 12 digits of your account number as your password.

Sincerely,
Vijay Kumar
BetterBank Limited

Letter 2. A promotional offer

Dear Preferred Customer:

The festive season is here! It is time to celebrate but it is also the time to grow your wealth. As our Preferred Customer, we at BetterBank offer an opportunity that cannot be missed. Gold at cost!

Yes! We give you gold coins at cost without any commission. You can buy gold coins from 1 gm to 10 gm without paying the exorbitant commission that most banks charge.

Buy as many as you want—there is no limit! You can gift them to your loved ones or keep them as a hedge against inflation.

As always, we are there for you. We look forward to building a lasting relationship with you.

Yours Sincerely
Ajay Kumar
Vice-President Relationship Division
BetterBank
For further details, contact your nearest BetterBank branch. Conditions apply.

Purpose and Audience

Genres present information in different ways because their audience differs. In the example below, the same information is given in a tourist brochure and an encyclopaedia. How does their language differ?

Tourist brochure

Nestling in the foothills of the Himalayas is the idyllic village of Silampur. This unspoiled spot offers the perfect escape from your hectic city life. Walk through enticing orchards of plums, apricots, and peaches. Wander through enchanting fields of flowers—roses, carnations, and hydrangeas. And if you are up for exercise, you can go boating on an exquisite lake in the heart of the village. The weather is perfect either to cool off in summer or to huddle around a log fire in winter. Silampur is just a hop, skip and jump from the plains—take the train to Haldwani and then it's a short taxi ride to the village.

Encyclopaedia entry

> Silampur is in the foothills of the Himalayas in the state of Uttarakhand, about 150 km from Haldwani, the nearest train station. The average temperature during the year is 15 to 20 degrees centigrade, dropping to 0 during winter. The population is 2,000. The main occupations are farming and horticulture, mainly for markets in Delhi. The water supply comes from a small reservoir.

Differences between the texts

The tourist brochure tries to persuade people to visit a certain destination, so is written from the perspective of a visitor; in contrast, the encyclopaedia entry aims to inform the reader and is neutral. The table below shows differences in the words and phrases they use.

Tourist brochure	**Encyclopaedia entry**
a short taxi ride to the village	150 km from Haldwani
cool off in summer	15 to 20 degrees centigrade
huddle around a log fire in winter	0 in winter
lake	reservoir
plums, apricots, and peaches	agriculture
roses, carnations, and hydrangeas	horticulture

There are other differences in the words used. The brochure uses subjective adjectives that cannot be independently verified—*unspoiled, enticing, enchanting, exquisite, perfect, short.* In contrast, the adjectives in the encyclopaedia entry can be verified—*nearest, main, average, small.*

Newspapers, Reports, and Research Articles

Here are three paragraphs from a newspaper article, a report, and a research paper. Can you identify which is which and how do you know? Highlight the words and sentences that helped you decide.

1. The West throws tremendous sums of money at innovation, but in India we rely on *jugaad*—a quick fix using everyday materials. Does the door of your new refrigerator squeak? You don't need to wait for a replacement from the company. The service engineer can fix that annoying squeak with talcum powder. Multinational companies are learning from India how to do more with less, stripping the bells and whistles from their over-engineered products and offering customers the basics. This is sweet music to the ears of consumers because prices go down. But does this really help the consumer? In the long run, *jugaad* or frugal innovation is only about bringing down

costs. It doesn't lead to inventions, and so people are stuck with the same old products held together with string.

2. The period from 2000 to 2009 witnessed substantial growth in the number of school-goers in the country. A comparison of school-goers in 2000 and 2009 reveals increased participation in both primary and secondary education in every state (see Figure 1). The largest increase was in the Union Territories and Kerala; in other states, the median for retention in school rose by around 1.3 years.
3. Student writers, and non-native writers in particular, find it difficult to structure their introductions in a manner that makes the text coherent to the reader. Their problem arises from two sources: the structuring of discourse and the overall structure of the introduction. Discourse, especially expository prose, is organised both hierarchically and linearly, i.e., the text is arranged hierarchically but the sentences are written (and read) linearly (Hinds 1979). At the same time, introductions have an overall structure that appears to be specific to introductions and is treated as such in textbooks. Textbooks such as Oshima and Hogue (1991: 78–79) describe the overall structure as a funnel, with the most general introduction at the beginning, gradually narrowing in level of generality until it ends with the specific research question that will be tackled in the body of the paper. A potential problem with student writers that has been noted by Wilkinson (1991) is the choice of end-points in this funnel: they may begin with information that is too general (given the audience) or they may become too specific towards the end of the introduction, by going into the details of the paper.

Solution

1. Report
2. Newspaper article
3. Research paper

The language used in these three texts differs. How many differences can you identify? Use the table below to list the differences.

Feature	**Newspaper article**	**Report**	**Research paper**
Personal pronouns			
Verbs			
Adjectives			
Metaphors			
Contracted forms			
Rhetorical questions			
Technical terms			
References to other material			

Intensifiers			
Hedges			
Sentence length & complexity			

Solution

Feature	**Newspaper article**	**Report**	**Research paper**
Personal pronouns	we, you	x	x
Verbs	throws, squeak, stuck, stripping, fix	to be, static verbs like witnessed, revealed	to be, static verbs like find, make, arise
Adjectives	annoying	x	x
Metaphors	bells and whistles, sweet music to the ears	x	x
Contracted forms	don't	x	x
Rhetorical questions	does this really help the consumer?	x	x
Technical terms	x	x	discourse, expository, hierarchically, coherent
References to other material	x	Refers to material within the document– see Figure 1	Refers to external sources: Hinds 1979, Oshima and Hogue (1991: 78-79), Wilkinson (1991)
Intensifiers	tremendous	x	x
Hedges	x	x	appears to be, may
Sentence length & complexity	short sentences, some complex sentences	short sentences, all complex	long sentences, all complex

The three types of texts have different styles because they address different audiences and serve different purposes. The table below shows some of these differences.

Feature	Newspaper article	Report	Research paper
Tone	Friendly, persuasive	Formal, informing	Knowledgeable, arguing a case
Idioms, metaphors, slang	Yes	No	No
Technical terms	No	No	Yes
Authority	More than reader	Much more than reader	Attempts to convince peers

Newspaper articles

The reader scans a newspaper, looking for something interesting. Hence, the language is catchy and uses clever turns of phrase, slang, metaphors, and idioms. There are no technical terms; if any are used, they are explained in layperson's terms.

Reports

The reader is looking for accurate and comprehensive information on a specific topic. Reports are intended to be authoritative and available to a wide audience.

Reports adopt a straightforward and clear style. They avoid slang, idioms and metaphors because these have nuances that might complicate the message; further, they might be lost on readers with weak English proficiency. Technical terms, if used, are explained in the text; jargon is avoided because the report tries to reach a wide audience.

Reports are clearly structured, with headings and sub-headings that make it easy to locate information. For the same reason, paragraphs have topic sentences, so that readers can skim through the material, skipping what they already know.

Reports aim to be a standalone document that is complete in itself. Many reports include figures and tables, but there are few footnotes or references to external sources. If there are references to external sources, these are usually given as end-notes for readers who want to check other sources.

Research paper

The academic research paper is not written for the public but addresses a small group of readers who specialise (or hope to specialise) in the research area. The relationship between the writer and reader is complex; the writer cannot merely inform this group of experts, but has to present a convincing argument using the paradigms, terms, and literature of the discipline.

Throughout the paper, the writer must convey the impression of objectivity, so that the argument appears reasonable. This is done through neutral language: there are no extreme statements. In fact, researchers use a high number of hedges (such as might, indicates, and sometimes) to qualify their statements.

Research papers rarely use short or simple sentences. Complex sentences are used because they allow the writer to qualify statements, include exceptions, provide references, etc. which are necessary for sophisticated argumentation. Further, this is possible because the audience is highly literate and familiar with concepts and theories in the field.

One marked feature of academic papers is the use of numerous references to external sources, usually other research papers in the field. This is often used to establish the writer's credibility by displaying knowledge of current work in the area. Another feature is the use of technical terms that are known to the insider group and often require no explanation (unless it is controversial and a working definition is required).

Informal vs. Formal Language

Reports are designed to be informative and academic papers are written to advance knowledge in the field. To establish their credibility, these genres use formal vocabulary and sentence structures. In fact, academic language is sometimes so formal that it can be impenetrable. However, the other extreme is an informal style that uses slang, metaphors, and idioms. Unless you are a journalist, avoid informal language in an academic paper, because you undercut the seriousness of your claims.

You can find a list of frequently used academic words at the following website and download it for your reference:
`http://language.massey.ac.nz/staff/awl/frequent.shtml`

Below, you can see how we change informal language to more formal language.

Informal language	**Formal language**
Expert systems can *help out* in the diagnosis of problems.	Expert systems can *assist* in the diagnosis of problems.
Radiation levels have been *going up and down.*	Radiation levels have been *fluctuating.*

EXERCISES

Q1. This text has been written for a layperson. Convert it into a factual piece for an encyclopaedia.

Were there dinosaurs in India? Of course there were dinosaurs in India! Many dinosaur bones, eggs, and nests have been found in India, but not many people know about Indian dinosaurs.

People who find a dinosaur get to name it, and so Indian dinosaurs have very interesting names that you can understand—names like Jainosaurus and Jubbulpuria. Here are some Indian dinosaurs. Try to guess their names! Hint: *saurus* means lizard and *suchus* means crocodile.

One Indian dinosaur is the Indosuchus. It's easy to guess what the name means: Indian crocodile. Its remains were found in Madhya Pradesh. This one was a meat-eater. It was twice the height of a man and about 6 meters long, with a crested skull that was flattened on the top. The Dravidosaurus, another Indian dinosaur, means Dravidian lizard because it was found in Tamil Nadu. It ate plants, was as tall as a man and 3 metres long. We don't know what the head looked like, because the skull has not been found. Kotasaurusmeans Kota lizard. It was twice as tall as a man and 9 metres long. Another vegetarian!

Other Indian dinosaurs have more unusual names. Barapasaurus Tagorei means big leg lizard (bara = big, pa = foot, Tagorei = Rabindranath Tagore) and was found in Andhra Pradesh. This dinosaur certainly had a big foot! Its height to its hip was about 5.5 metres, which is the height of three people. And it managed this size even though it ate only plants. The strangest name is the one given to the Isisaurus. This dinosaur was named after the Indian Statistical Institute (ISI). So, the name means ISI lizard!Although this dinosaur ate only plants, it was 18 metres long and weighed 15,000 kg.

Q2. Read the letter from Ranjan to his friend, Mithali. Use the information to compose a letter from Ranjan to his supervisor, Ajay Pal. Your letter should extract the relevant information and present it in a formal style.

Hi Mithali:
How's the new job going? Hope they appreciate your skills there!

Guess whom I ran into the other day—Subir Nag from our M.A class! We caught up over lunch and laughed over old times. He now heads the e-Learning division at a company called Ficus Ltd. Who would have thought he had it in him! He seems to be handling a lot: creating e-Learning courses for Indian and Australian universities. Would you believe that 200 people report to him? Apparently, e-Learning requires a lot of staff, so he has instructional designers, graphics artists and programmers working on these projects. And then they have project managers who see that everything goes according to schedule. I think this may be the answer to our company's prayer—we are supposed to get 'with it' and 'do' e-Learning and don't have a clue where to begin. Maybe I can get them to convert our face-to-face training into e-Learning courses—and I can snap up a bonus!

We're meeting at his office on Friday, so that he can impress me with the corner office and personal secretary (not to mention the coffee machine).

Catch up with you some time. Does lunch next week sound good?

Ranjan

Q3. Go to the texts in Section 3.

1. Re-write the newspaper paragraph so that it reads like a piece of academic writing.
2. Turn the report into a newspaper article.

Q4. Find formal alternatives for the words in italics in the sentences.

1. Internet use will *go up* when telephone rates are reduced.
2. Research expenditures have *gone up* to nearly $350 million.
3. The software will *let you* create 3D images.
4. Long simulation time is *needed.*
5. Encryption software helps *stop* the theft of personal data.
6. In this project, I will *try* to develop a wheelchair robot.
7. *Many* bubbles cluster and change shape.
8. *More and more* people are joining the workforce in India.
9. Let us *club* these factors under four headings.
10. Several schools are facing a staff *crunch.*
11. Researchers have *found out* that this drug is dangerous.
12. Solar energy will *remove* the energy problem.
13. Several studies have been *cranked out* in the area of cultural schemata.

Q5. The sentences below have been taken from research reports, which should use formal language. Change the informal language to a more formal style.

1. For starters, India has an enormous pool of English speakers.
2. The two Presidents set the ball rolling for Indo-Japanese relations.
3. The country is India's main competitor and this fact cannot be wished away.
4. The revised offers by the competitors are pretty restrictive.
5. India has never rolled out the welcome mat for foreign companies.
6. If the government does not change its policy, the chances of getting re-elected will be zero.
7. For the time being, the issue should be put on the back burner.
8. The company was in no way going to be given the project.
9. India should guard against going overboard with hype and hopes about the relationship with the US.
10. In 2007, India was seen as a hot number for private equity firms.
11. The clothing company is not really bothered about working conditions at the factory as long as the product meets their quality standards.
12. The US only sat up and took serious note of India when the Indian economy was liberalised in the 1990s.

ANSWERS

1. Indian dinosaurs

    1. **Indosuchus** Meaning: Indian crocodile: Habitat: Found in Madhya Pradesh Description: Carnivore, 4 metres tall and 6 metres long. Crested skull that was flattened on top.
    2. **Dravidosaurus** Meaning: Dravidian lizard Habitat: Found in Tamil Nadu Description: Herbivore, 2 metres tall, 3 metres long. Skull has not been found.
    3. **Kotasaurus** Meaning: Kota lizard Description: Herbivore, 4 metres tall, 9 metres long.
    4. **Barapasaurus Tagorei** Meaning: Big leg lizard. Habitat: Found in Andhra Pradesh Description: Herbivore, height to hip around 5.5 metres.
    5. **Isisaurus** Meaning: This dinosaur was named after the Indian Statistical Institute (ISI). Habitat: Found in Maharashtra Description: Herbivore, 18 metres long, weighed 15,000 kg.

2. Dear Mr Pal,

    As part of our e-Learning endeavour, I met Mr Nag who heads the e-Learning division at Ficus Ltd., which has the experience and resources to convert our face-to-face training into e-Learning courses. The company has already created e-Learning courses for Indian and Australian universities. Further, they have a staff of 200 people—project managers, instructional designers, graphics artists, and programmers—who should be able to handle our requirements.

    I have set up another appointment with Mr Nag this week, where I will discuss the company's capabilities in further detail. If they can handle our requirements, I suggest that we ask them to create a prototype.

    With regards
    Ranjan Kumar

3.
    1. From a newspaper to a research article
    Although *jugaad* appears to offer benefits to the consumer, in the long run it does not lead to the invention of new products.
    2. From a report to a newspaper
    For decades, pessimists about school education have had a field day decrying the sorry state of the educational system. But it may be time to cheer. School education in Indian states is showing remarkable results. In the new century, more and more students joined school in all states. Happily, this was not only in primary schools but also in secondary schools. Even better, this did not happen only in the states where we expect it. Certainly, the Union Territories and Kerala came ahead, but the news was still good in other states, with children staying in school for around $1\frac{1}{2}$ years longer.

4.
    1. Internet use will *increase* when telephone rates are reduced.
    2. Research expenditures have *risen* to nearly $350 million.
    3. The software will *allow* you to create 3D images.

4. Long simulation time is *required.*
5. Encryption software helps *prevent* the theft of personal data.
6. In this project, I will *attempt* to develop a wheelchair robot.
7. *Several* bubbles cluster and change shape.
8. *Increasing numbers of* people are joining the workforce in India.
9. Let us *group* these factors under four headings.
10. Several schools are facing a staff *shortage.*
11. Researchers have *determined* that this drug is dangerous.
12. Solar energy will *eliminate* the energy problem.
13. Several studies have been *conducted* in the area of cultural schemata.

5. 1. *To begin with,* India has an enormous pool of English speakers.
2. The two Presidents *initiated* Indo-Japanese relations.
3. The country is India's main competitor and this fact cannot be *ignored.*
4. The revised offers by the competitors are *restrictive.*
5. India has never *welcomed* foreign companies.
6. If the government does not change its policy, there will be *no chance* of getting re-elected.
7. For the time being, the issue should be put *aside.*
8. The company was not going to be given the project *under any circumstances.*
9. India should guard against *becoming too optimistic* about the relationship with the US.
10. In 2007, India was seen as a *popular option* for private equity firms.
11. The clothing company is not *interested* in working conditions at the factory as long as the product meets their quality standards.
12. The US only *became interested* in India when the Indian economy was liberalised in the 1990s.

CHAPTER 9

Writing Reports

INTRODUCTION

Reports are part of a science student's life. In subjects such as physics, chemistry and biology, we do experiments, record the results, and then write a laboratory report about what we did. Today, reports are found everywhere—in business organisations, in NGOs, in government institutions, and in universities. Hence, even school students are being taught report writing.

In Chapter 8, we looked at the differences among three genres—newspaper articles, reports, and research papers. Of the three, reports are the easiest to write because reports are factual. In a newspaper article or research report, you have to think of an original idea and defend your argument; these are argumentative texts. In a report, you merely report information that you or other people recorded; this is primarily an expository text.

What is a report? A report does just that—it reports. It is a factual and informative text about what happened. The model of a report is the laboratory report from your school days or a police report. They are accurate, brief, and complete accounts backed by evidence and are written in a neutral style without your personal opinion or the word 'I'.

TYPES OF REPORTS

Books on business communication and technical writing deal with various sub-types of reports—formal, semi-formal, and informal reports, long versus short reports, internal reports versus consultants' reports, etc. There appears to be tremendous variety in reports, but in fact there are only two types of reports depending on the purpose of the report.

The Documentation Report

These reports document what was done. They are used to monitor progress and to maintain a record of the action taken and money spent.

> **Example**
> An NGO received funding from the agency to conduct an educational programme. The NGO has to write progress reports and a final report so that the agency can determine if the money was wisely spent. Such reports can be used to apply for further funds.

The Assessment Report

These reports assess a situation before action is taken.

> **Example**
> A funding agency wants to invest in education in India. It needs information on the status of education, the different models, and the most appropriate method and segment for investment. It asks for a report on the status of education in India.

Such reports gather information on a specific situation and often contain a section on recommendations. Their purpose is to help decision makers arrive at a decision. They are frequently written by or for business organisations, government organisations, the United Nations (UN) and the World Bank. They could be for internal circulation (as in a business organisation) or for wider dissemination to laypeople (as with the UN). Depending on the complexity of the situation, their length can vary from 20 pages to 800 pages.

Format of a Report

Unlike research papers, there is no common format for reports. Organisations usually have their own templates and these vary across organisations. In general, the audience and purpose dictate the format of the report—from the number of pages down to the page layout.

Here is a short documentation report that illustrates the main features of a report. Look at the comments in the left column. Then do Exercise 2 at the end of the chapter.

Title	**Update on English Proficiency Course in Shiksha College, Punjab University** Prepared by Dr V.K. Varma, Course Director
Context and Purpose given	As part of the initiatives to re-design the English curriculum, this report describes the English Proficiency Course (EPC) conducted in Shiksha College and recommends specific actions.

<table>
<tr><td>Numbered headings
Relevant facts given</td><td>1. Course implementation
A diagnostic test was conducted on February 1, 2016 at the college (Appendix A). Of the 61 students who took the test, 30 students were selected; their scores on the test ranged from 40% to 70%. The students were divided into two groups: Class A and Class B.</td></tr>
<tr><td>Additional information given in appendices</td><td>The course ran from February 4 to March 11, 2016 with 32 hours of classroom instruction. The classes were held from 2 p.m. to 4 p.m. three times a week – Monday, Wednesday and Saturday. At the end of the course, students took a final test (Appendix B).

The classes were taught by Priya Roy (Class A) and Tasleem Hussein (Class B), who are full-time faculty at the college. Both teachers have MA degrees in English literature, but Ms Hussein also has a certificate in language teaching. The classes were observed by Meera Sirkar, head of the English department.

The pre- and post-test scores for each student are given in Appendix C. Of the 30 participants, only 15 showed an improvement in their scores.

2. Course content
The course emphasised the spoken skills. Teachers were given a list of sub-skills, such as reading a poem out loud (Appendix D), but were free to design their own activities.

3. Results
When the student scores were analysed, it was found that students in Class B performed better on the final test on spoken language.</td></tr>
<tr><td>Based on data</td><td>4. Recommendations
These recommendations are based on an examination of student scores, classroom observation, and faculty feedback.

The difference in scores can be attributed to the different teaching methods employed. Students in Class B were given extensive practice in speaking during class, whereas students in Class A listened to lectures by the teacher.</td></tr>
<tr><td>Numbered sub-sections

with different formatting</td><td>4.1 Teacher qualifications. A strong background in language teaching is necessary. Teachers who do not have a teaching certificate tend to lecture and do not encourage student participation.

4.2 Course content. Teachers may be unable to devise their own activities; hence, the content of the course and the activities should be clearly laid out and teachers told to follow them.</td></tr>
</table>

	4.3 Teacher training. Since teachers are paid extra for conducting the classes, several teachers were interested in teaching the classes. The university should consider running certificate courses to train faculty in teaching English in order to meet the shortfall.
Information in lists	**5. Impact of the project** The project shows that students' language proficiency improves when they are taught by trained English teachers. Given the increasing demand for English proficiency courses and the vast pool of English literature teachers, the university should investigate ways to tap this market. For this, the following needs to be done: • Design English courses and textbooks that emphasise language skills rather than literature. • Re-vamp existing English courses so that they cater to workplace literacy. • Train faculty to conduct these courses, both in the short-term and as part of the BA/MA curriculum.
Additional information	**Attachments** • Appendix A. Diagnostic test • Appendix B. Final test • Appendix C. Student scores on Pre-Test and Post-Test • Appendix D. List of sub-skills

Assessment Reports

Assessment reports provide an in-depth analysis of a situation, sometimes with recommended actions. They have become a necessary genre due to the high volume of information. In situations where people have to make decisions, such as business or government organisations, a team of people gather up-to-date information, select what is pertinent to the situation, and present it in a report to the decision-makers. There is no room for 'perhaps' and 'maybe'; instead, there needs to be a high level of certainty so that action can be taken.

To make the information accessible to different levels of readers, the information is structured in layers. The Executive Summary is only one page written in bullet points, which summarises the main findings and the recommended actions; this is for the busy CEO, who may not read further. Important information in the text is boxed; detailed tables, statistical analyses, and lists of people are moved to the Appendix for people down the line who want to check the accuracy of the data or replicate the study.

Most assessment reports are not written by an individual but by a team, because of the amount of data that has to be collected and sifted. Because of the vast amount of work that it entails, most reports are not available to the general public but have to be bought. However, it is possible to view sample reports to get an idea of how such reports are written and structured.

Writing a Report

A report should be accurate, brief and complete. The Economist Intelligence Unit (EIU) shows how they write their reports and this is a useful guide.

1. *Accurate.* The information and data is reliable and up-to-date.
2. *Brief.* Since you don't have to build argument, you merely give the facts. However, this is not an information dump; you have to offer insights into the issues or recommendations.
3. *Complete.* Within a report, all the relevant information is given. It is a standalone document. The reader should not have to hunt for additional documents or information.

Common Problems

Writing a report sounds straightforward: gather the facts, organise them, and write them clearly. What could go wrong? Plenty! Here are some common problems.

Too long

When researchers are paid a lot of money to write a report, they feel they need to provide value for money; however, instead of adding insights, they add pages to the report. Remember that less is more: it is easier to keep adding pages than to distil the main ideas.

Report padding is done in different ways; check your reports for these padding strategies.

(a) Explain every figure

> Figure 2 compares mobile phone use in India and China from the year 2000 to date. The figure shows that in India, mobile phone use increased from the year 2000 to 2001, dipped in the year 2003, but picked up again in 2004 from where it continued to rise steadily. In contrast, usage has grown at a steady rate in China from the year 2000 to date.

Why include a figure if you have to explain it in detail?

(b) Describe the data in detail

> During the survey, one participant said, 'My grandson has shown me that a mobile phone has many features. He knows a lot because he studies in an English-medium school and is a very clever boy. He showed me how to take pictures and...

This is interesting to the researcher who spent hours in the field; however, it does not move the report forward.

(c) Historical perspective

> The mobile service has seen phenomenal growth since 2000. India's mobile phone subscriber base grew exponentially from around 10 million in 2002 to 350 million by the start of 2009.

How does this help the reader in the year 2017? Don't include a historical narrative unless you are writing a history of the field.

Too many researchers

It is said that a camel is a horse that has been designed by a committee. We find this problem in a report written by several project members; each person wants his or her section to be included. As the report moves to senior levels, people add information instead of subtracting it. This results in a 'lumpy' report.

A Biased Report

A company asks you to write a report about their competitors. You know they would love to see a report that criticises the competition, but such a report is not objective and undermines your credibility in future projects.

Remember,

1. Be accurate, brief, and complete.
2. Use a direct and informative style. Be factual. Don't use adjectives or emotive words.
3. Report facts, supported by data. Move references and sources for footnotes, endnotes.
4. Save your opinion for the recommendations.

EXERCISES

Q1. Below you will find scenarios requiring reports. Decide which ones require an assessment report and which needs a documentation report.

1. Your team sets up an online examination for an organisation. When you return to your company, you describe the successes, problems and money spent.
2. A university wants to update its curriculum. It decides to examine the gaps and deficiencies in the current curriculum, examine what other universities are doing and what stakeholders want, and assess alternatives.
3. Country X is known for its orchids. Is there a market for this in India and, if so, what are the constraints? Whom do they contact?
4. Your college trials a new language programme for one year. During the year, you provide ongoing reports about the progress of the programme
5. As the project manager, you visit the factory site and meet with the site manager and construction team. When you return, you write up the progress and problems at the site.
6. A company wants to set up a factory in State X. What are the opportunities and blocks? The trade representative meets distributors in India. She sends a report on the level of interest in the product.
7. A company sees an opportunity to set up an examination system in India. It needs a report on the status and the opportunities: what is the current system, where are the gaps, who are the competitors, etc.

Q2. 1. Why do reports use subheadings?
2. Why do reports use lists?
3. Why is additional information given in appendices and not in the main text?

Q3. On the Internet, try to find and download some sample reports from the following.

- Economist Intelligence Unit (EIU)
- United Nations Human Development Reports
- Central Square Foundation

Identify the features of these reports and find the ones you would like to emulate in your own writing. Here are some features you may want to compare and study.

- Length. How long are the reports and why?
- Executive Summary vs. Abstract. Which one is longer? Which is more complete? Why?
- Acronyms or Abbreviations. Why is this necessary?
- Table of Contents. What does the Table of Contents include? How is it formatted? What numbering is used?
- Layout. Notice the location of subheadings, use of boxes and colour, etc.
- Footnotes and Endnotes. Which one is used and why?
- Tables and Figures. How are they formatted? What is the numbering system?
- Appendices. What do they contain? How are they numbered?
- References or Bibliography. Why is it included?
- Glossary. If there is a glossary, what does it contain? When is it necessary?

Q4. A phone company is considering whether to incorporate Indian scripts in its phones. You are part of the research team. A member of the team has produced the following Executive Summary. Re-write the summary by extracting the important information and using bullet points. Your Executive Summary should not be more than one page.

Market for Non-English Phones in India

With a mobile subscriber base of 525 million in December 2009, India is second only to China in the size of its mobile phone market. The mobile service has seen phenomenal growth since 2000. India's mobile phone subscriber base grew exponentially from around 10 million in 2002 to 350 million by the start of 2009. A whopping 19 million subscriber are added each month.

Several factors have contributed to this amazing growth, such as low tariffs and stiff competition in the market. These changes are relatively recent; until the 1990s, telephone connections were the monopoly of the government with 10-year waiting lists, but this changed when the field was thrown open to private players. Calls across India are among the cheapest in the world.

India represents a growing market for the mobile phone industry. It is growing at a staggering rate with a population of 1.2 billion, rising incomes and growing consumerism, and its vast geography. It is also a youthful country; more than half the population is under the age of 24. The density of mobile phone users in India is 8.5 for every 100 people and India's rural mobile phone users have crossed the 100 million mark. At the same time, it presents challenges due to the low literacy rate of 64% and the number of languages and scripts that are used for communication.

Mobile phones not only offer users calling facilities, but also facilities to transfer text and images. Most mobile phones come equipped with cameras and Internet faculties. However, these are under-utilised because the instruments and software are only in English.

This report examines the feasibility of introducing Indian language phones in the Indian market. The report is based on research reports from government and business organisations, as well as a primary survey of 1,000 users from different socio-economic backgrounds living in cities (Tier I, Tier II, and Tier III) and rural areas.

Although English is known and used by many Indians, these form a small proportion of the population. There are over 400 languages in India, of which 22 language have official status. These languages are written in a variety of scripts. Nine scripts are derived from the ancient script of Brahmi and, although their symbols differ, they follow the same logic for forming characters. A tenth script used for the language, Urdu, is derived from the Arabic/Persian script.

Our survey found that the urban middle-class groups used mobile phones for a variety of purposes—social networking, downloading jokes and horoscopes, etc. However, other groups used phones primarily for talking to friends or for work. This is changing among the rural population; for example, many farmers use mobile phones to get updated prices for their produce. However, they have to rely on voice data since they are either illiterate or they cannot understand the English text.

Many users are familiar with the English alphabet since it is one of the languages taught in school. However, they would prefer a device that uses their language as this would speed up their tasks. In the absence of such devices, they work around the constraints. For example, they type messages in an Indian language using the English keys; the receiver views the message in the Indian language written in the English alphabet; both sender and receiver need to know the English script. Another solution is to use software that converts English key strokes into the Indian script. However, both sender and receiver need the same software. In both cases, English is the channel through which messages are sent and received; this is clearly not an optimal solution for users. Even users who do not send text messages face problems reading the menu options and instructions which are in English; their solution is to memorise a sequence so that they call place calls. This is also the case with illiterate users; there is a high number of them as the literacy rate in India is only 64%.

When users were asked what they would like to see in a phone, they mentioned that the menu and instructions should be given in their script. Those who want to send messages would also like the keys and display to be in their script. When asked about the need for a manual, the majority said that they never read manuals; instead the user interface should be intuitive.

Discussions with software companies revealed that it is possible to design and implement software for the 10 scripts. The best option is a single algorithm for all nine Indic scripts that could be customised for each script; this is possible given that the nine scripts differ only in their symbols. For Urdu, which is written from right-to-left, existing software for Farsi (from which it is derived) can be used.

ANSWERS

1. Assessment reports: 2, 3, 6, 7
   Documentation reports: 1, 4, 5
2. 1. Subheadings act as a guide to the content and make the structure easy to follow.
   2. Lists create a visual impact and make important information stand out.
   3. The text should flow smoothly; hence, any information that is necessary but interrupts the flow is given in a separate section at the end called an Appendix. The specialist can refer to the Appendix; other readers can skip it.

3. **Market for Non-English Phones in India**

- The mobile phone base was 525 million at the end of December 2009, and grows at 19 million per month.
- English is used primarily by the urban middle class in India. Hence, English-only phones do not meet the needs of a large portion of the consumer base.
- Our survey found that non-English users memorise a sequence of steps in order to handle phone calls. Those who know the English script type the message in an Indian language using the English alphabet; depending on the software, the display is either in the English script or in an Indian script (however, the receiver must have the same software to view the message).
- Many people are illiterate. The literacy rate is only 64% and mobile phones are primarily used for talking to people. However, phones are now being used to get updates on prices (as in the case of farmers), so text entry and display in Indian scripts offers a market opportunity.
- Nine scripts used to write the Indian languages; another script, Urdu, is based on the Arabic script.

Recommendations
The size of the potential market warrants phones that use Indic scripts.

- Potential users are the urban poor, and residents of Tier III cities and rural areas.
- A single algorithm can handle 14 Indic scripts; for Urdu, software for Arabic or Farsi can be used.
- The scripts should be used for the menu, instructions, keys, and text display. There is no need for a manual in the Indian languages.

CHAPTER 10

Writing a Short Research Paper

INTRODUCTION

Writing a research paper is very different from answering examination questions. First, the answer is not available in a textbook; instead, you have to provide an original paper that will contribute to the field in some small way. Second, a research paper is usually based on data; in most cases, you collect your own data, but you can also draw on large datasets, such as the Census of India. Third, unlike a timed examination, you are given time to write a research paper; this could be one month or the entire semester. And since you have time, you are expected to submit a professional document that has gone through several revisions.

In this chapter, you will learn how to write a short 4-page research paper. This is the norm in several international universities, where BA students submit such papers, often as a final thesis.

UNDERSTANDING THE TEXT

To understand the steps in writing a research paper, we will select a small topic and work with that.

What makes a city liveable?

Countries have begun to assess the quality of their cities and cities are now ranked on how liveable they are, but citizens may have their own ideas about what makes a city liveable. This is what you will find out for this paper.

- What factors do the studies consider?
- What factors are important to students in your college?
- Is there a difference?

Since research work is usually a collaborative effort involving several researchers, we will replicate this practice. You should work in groups of three and then submit individual papers for your grade. In the Appendix, you will find a sample research paper that can help you understand the sections and the language used in a research paper.

There are two main steps in writing a research paper: (a) collecting data and (b) writing the paper.

1. **Collecting data**. This is group work. First, you get an overview of the area by looking up information on the Internet to see what people have studied and found. Then you design a short questionnaire and ask 30 people for their opinions. When you have the responses, the group will summarise the data in a table and create a bar chart.
2. **Writing the paper**. This is individual work. You have the data and so you can begin writing the paper. The paper should be 2-4 pages, 1.5 spacing. The main sections are given in Figure 10.1.

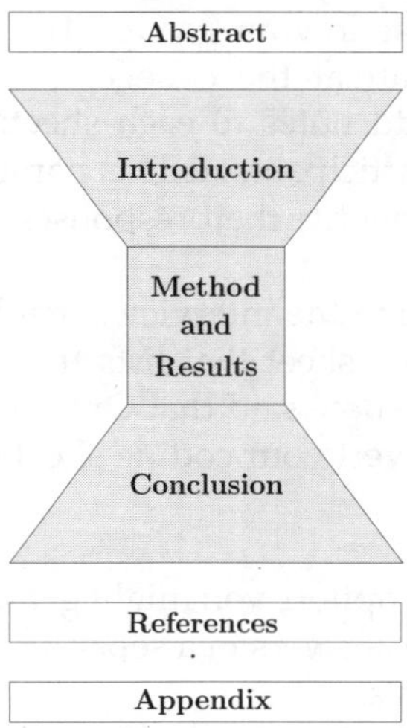

Figure 10.1: Sections of the research paper

At the end of this chapter, you will find a sample research paper that uses hypothetical data. While you are writing your research paper, check how this is done in the sample.[1]

Data Collection

Overview of the Field

Find articles, reports and news items on the topic. This was covered in Chapter 3, which discussed how to gather information before writing a paper. Look for information on why

[1]Note for the Instructor: If students come from different disciplines, I usually ask them to photocopy a research article in their discipline and use that as a sample.

this topic is important, what studies have found and what criteria they used. Write down the references. You will use this information when you write the Introduction.

Start thinking about your questionnaire. Look at the criteria that studies have used. Do you want to use these criteria or different ones?

Collect Data

The first step is to design a short questionnaire to help you get information on your research question. You can be lazy and ask an open-ended question such as 'What do you think makes a city liveable?', but students may not know where to start. It is better to give them a list of options and ask, 'Which one is the most important to you?' Include a category called 'Other' that may trigger some interesting responses.

When the questionnaire is ready, you will have to interview 30 people. Split the interviews among the three people in your group. The participants will be students, but you could include faculty or staff at the college. It is worth printing copies of your questionnaire so that you can add notes to each sheet; include the date and time, and relevant information about the participant, such as name, gender, and home town. If you have the category 'Other', you can write their responses on this sheet.

When you have finished conducting the interviews, get back together and summarise the responses. Create a simple coding sheet that lists the options and count the number of responses for each option. If 12 people said that Option 1 was the most important, put 12 in the cell for Option 1. Then, convert your coding sheet into a bar chart, so that it is easier to visualise the data.

If you offer participants an 'Other' option, you might get some interesting responses that are not on your list. Summarise these answers in a separate section along with any interesting comments made by the participants.

WRITING THE PAPER

Now that you have the group data, each person can write up the research paper. The papers will look similar, but don't worry about that right now.

People get tempted to start by writing the Introduction. In fact, the Introduction is written last. We usually start with what we have in hand—the data. So, we begin by writing the Method and Results.

Write the Method Section

Your method section is ready and you can write it up. We use the past tense in this section because the work has been done.

In this section, you first describe the materials (what), participants (who), and procedure (how).

- **Materials**. Mention that you used a questionnaire and include a copy in the Appendix. Briefly explain why you chose certain options and not others.
- **Participants**. Describe the number of participants and their background. Were they students, faculty or workers? If they were students, which year were they studying in? You should give sufficient background on the participants, so that readers can say, 'Okay, this is true of first-year students in a Tier 2 town'. At the same time, you have to conceal the identity of your participants, so create different names for them.
- **Procedure**. Describe how you conducted the interviews. Write this as a walkthrough, so that readers can visualise step-by-step what participants did.

The next step is to describe how you analysed the data. In this study, you counted the number of responses for each option. However, you may have to drop some of the data. For example, if some participants gave unacceptable responses that you had to drop, mention this.

Write the Results Section

In this section, you report the findings from your data. Begin with a summary of the findings.

First, you report the numbers, which is called quantitative data. Your coding sheet will be too long and difficult for readers to understand, so this is where a figure helps. You have used the simplest figure for data—a bar chart—but research papers often provide tables for statistics, photographs of equipment, etc. You need to number your figures, e.g. Figure 1, Figure 2, etc. Direct the reader to the visual. Then, highlight the main trends and any significant numbers. Do not describe every number in tedious detail.

If you included an 'Other' category, you will have qualitative data. People will give widely differing responses and comments that are interesting but difficult to summarise. Researchers get tempted to include all this chatty information in their research paper, but it is exhausting for the reader. Pick out the most important or the most interesting information and give a few examples.

Discussion

In this section, you discuss what the data means. What do the numbers and responses tell us? Go back to the questions you raised at the beginning of the research project and see if you have answered the questions.

Write the Conclusion

This section begins with a summary of your study and then widens to the broader research area (see Figure 10.2). It uses a mixture of tenses: past tense for what is finished, present tense for general implications, and the future for further research. This section does not introduce new facts.

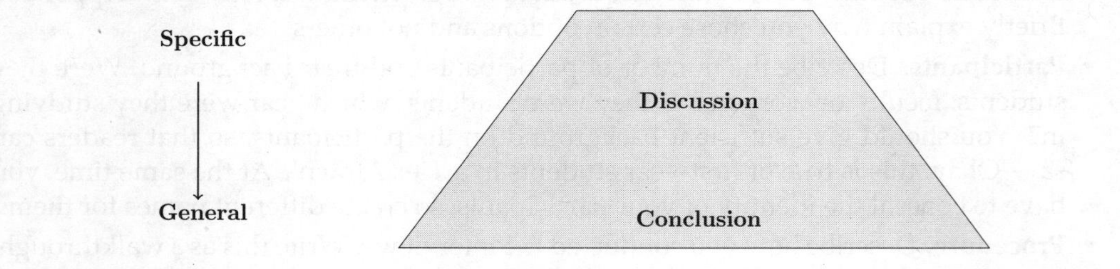

Figure 10.2: Discussion and conclusion of a research paper

1. State the purpose of the study.
   This study examined....
2. Summarise the main findings.
   The results show....
3. Propose future directions.
   Further research will examine...
   Two directions for future work are...

Write the Introduction and References

You are now ready to write the Introduction because you know what you want to say. The Introduction consists of four sections, which are shown in Figure 10.3.

1. Why the topic is important
2. What research has been done
3. What has not been done
4. What this paper will do

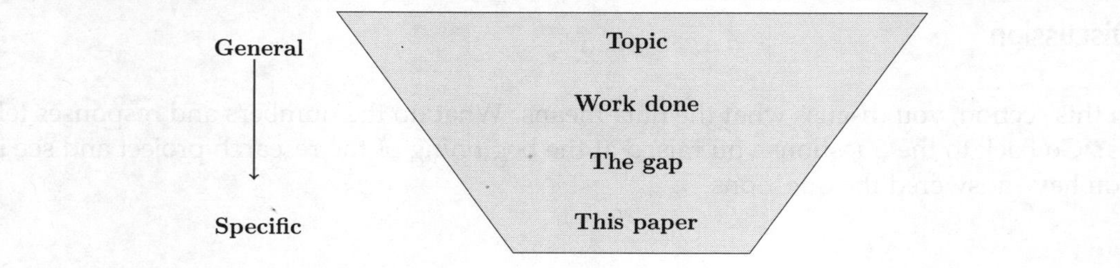

Figure 10.3: Introduction of a research paper

References are written in different ways in each discipline, and journals often have their own style. The sample paper uses the standard APA style from the American Psychological Association, which is commonly used for the social sciences.

Write the Abstract

This is the final section you will write. An abstract is a summary of the content of your paper that helps readers decide whether to read the paper.

The abstract is very short—between 150 and 250 words–and written as a single paragraph. At the same time, the abstract should be complete; the reader should be able to get the gist of your paper without reading the entire paper. The reason is that the abstract is frequently available to a wide audience through journal websites or collections of abstracts; researchers skim through thousands of abstracts, trying to decide which ones are relevant for their research. So, your abstract should allow the reader to decide whether to read your entire paper.

Although an abstract is only one paragraph, the following information is packed into it.

1. Background information. It provides the background to the problem. This is written in the present tense because it is still a problem.
2. Purpose of the study and its scope.
3. Method. How you collected and analysed the data.
4. Results. Most abstracts do not give the results; for the results, you have to get a copy of the paper.
5. Implications or recommendations

You have finished writing the first draft of your paper. The next step is to edit the language—check grammar and spelling— and proofread for errors.

APPENDIX: SAMPLE RESEARCH PAPER

Text Input on Different Devices in Different Scripts

Tomoko Izumita and Renu Gupta

Abstract

This study investigated ease of text entry on two devices—computers and mobile phones—in two scripts—English and Japanese. Subjects were 30 Japanese undergraduates at a computer science university. The variables were time taken and number of key presses. The results indicate that text entry is more difficult on mobile phones than on computers for both scripts, and require modifications to make them more user-friendly.

Introduction

In the past decade, electronic devices such as mobile phones, talking dictionaries, and computers have become easily available, but typing in non-alphabetic scripts can be a challenge and special programs have to be developed for users to type in these scripts (Scott Mackenzie and Tanaka-Ishii, 2007). For Indic scripts that are used in Asia, the programs have to incorporate algorithms that can combine symbols (as in Devanagari) and add tones (as in Thai) (Gupta and Sornlertlamvanich, 2007). For scripts such as Chinese and Japanese that use hundreds of characters, an Input Method Editor (IME) has to be included. This paper compares user performance in typing in two different scripts—English and Japanese—on two devices—a computer and a mobile phone—to identify problems in text entry.

Method

A short text in English was selected and translated into Japanese (see Appendix). The English text has more individual letters (232) than the Japanese text (122). However, typing the Japanese text is complicated (Hacker News), because it consists of syllables in hiragana, which are typed as a single letter, as well as kanji characters, which require a look-up in an IME (Figure 1).

Figure 1: Input method editor (IME)

The subjects were 30 second-year students in a bilingual computer science university in Japan. Their native language was Japanese, and they had been learning English for approximately 7 years. The students were proficient at typing on the computer in both Japanese and in English (which they used extensively for programming), and switched easily between the two scripts. On the mobile phone, they were proficient at typing in Japanese, which they used extensively for social media (such as Mixi).

The subjects worked in groups of three. They were told to type the two paragraphs (Japanese and English) on two devices (their workstation and their mobile phone) and record both the time taken and the number of key presses. In each group, one student did the typing, another student recorded the time taken, and the third student counted the number of key presses.

The data were collected from each group. It consisted of the time and number of key presses for each device. The mean time across groups on each variable was calculated. The data from one group was dropped because they were unable to enter text in their mobile phones.

Results

The results for the time taken are summarised in Figure 2. Subjects were able to type faster in Japanese than in English on both devices. However, the times are almost identical for typing in Japanese on the mobile phone (120 seconds) and in English on the workstation (125 seconds).

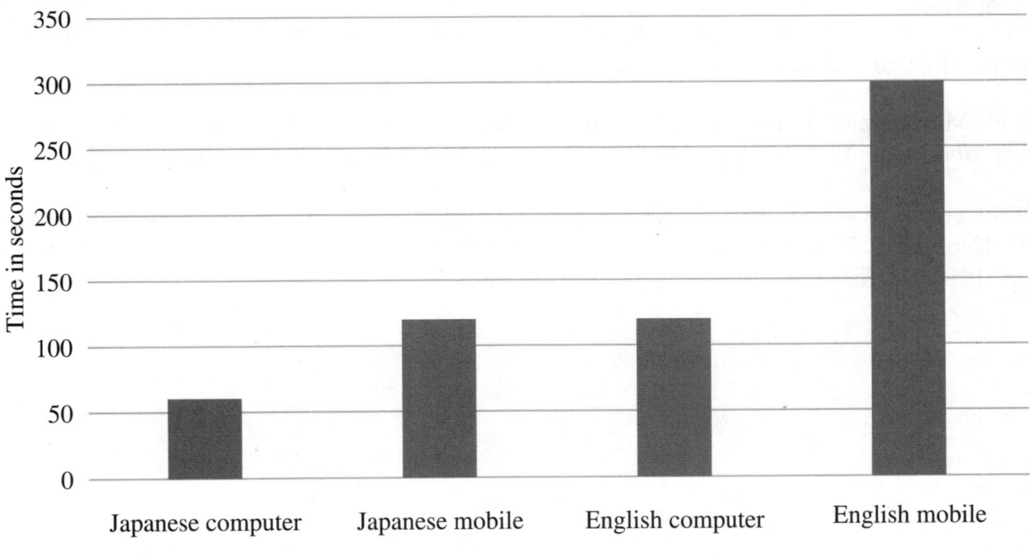

Figure 2: Time taken to type on 4 devices in 2 scripts

The data for key presses is not reported here because text entry in Japanese is complicated; although there are fewer individual letters (122 versus 232), selecting the correct option requires additional key presses, which was not calculated.

Discussion

There are several explanations for why subjects took longer to type English text on both the workstation and the mobile phone. The most obvious reason is lack of proficiency in the language; the presence of several low frequency and unfamiliar words in the English text (*paragraph, logically*) slowed down their typing. The second reason is the layout of the letters on the English mobile phone; subjects had to recall the alphabet sequence to find a letter, whereas this has been automatised in the case of Japanese.

The similar times for typing on the Japanese mobile phone and the English computer is surprising. This similarity may reflect the effects of practice, since the subjects are used to typing in English on the workstation for their programming assignments. It also suggests that the design of the Japanese mobile phone needs improvement.

Conclusion

This paper investigated the ease of typing on computers and mobile phones in two scripts—Japanese and English. The findings indicate that for Japanese users typing on the the mobile phone in either language is more difficult than typing on the computer. This difference could either be due to practice effects or to the cumbersome layout of the keys on the mobile phone, for which further studies are required.

Text entry on electronic devices requires key presses that may differ across devices and scripts. Although this feature has been noted (Hacker News) and we collected data on this variable, more systematic comparisons are required.

References

Hacker News. Available at https://news.ycombinator.com/item?id=12325844. Last accessed April 3, 2017.

Scott MacKenzie, I. and Tanaka-Ishii, K. (eds.) (2007). *Text Entry Systems: Mobility, Accessibility, Universality* (pp. 227-250). San Francisco: Morgan Kaufmann.

Tanaka-Ishii, K. and Gupta, R. (2007). Writing system variation and text entry. In I. Scott MacKenzie and K. Tanaka-Ishii (eds.), *Text Entry Systems: Mobility, Accessibility, Universality* (pp. 191-202). San Francisco: Morgan Kaufmann.

CHAPTER 11

More on the Research Paper

INTRODUCTION

This chapter is intended for researchers who need to write more than a simple term paper. In Chapter 10, I have discussed the basic components and steps in writing a research paper but this chapter, I will move to more advanced research papers and give examples of academic texts.

The process of formulating the research question, finding and reading the relevant papers, collecting and analysing the data, and finding worthwhile results is long and arduous. This book does not discuss this process; if you are a student, your supervisor is better able to see you through it, and if you have a PhD you have already been through this process. In this chapter, I assume that you have done your reading and research, and now need to write it up as a paper for publication or as a dissertation or thesis.

How long does it take to write a paper or thesis? Once you have your data and have read the relevant literature, you are hopefully clear about what you want to say. Then, writing the paper should take about one month of concentrated effort. However, if you are still exploring ideas through writing, it is going to take much, much longer.

This chapter is divided into two main sections:

1. Overview of a research paper: What it is and what can go wrong?
2. Sections of a research paper
   (a) The core sections: Introduction, Method, Results, Discussion, and Conclusion
   (b) Additional sections: Abstract, References, Acknowledgements, and Appendices

Some examples from research papers are given in the Appendices.

OVERVIEW OF A RESEARCH PAPER

The research paper is part of the academic tradition. It is normally written by university faculty, who conduct research and write up their findings in an article that they send to a research journal in their area of expertise. The paper is then reviewed by two or three experts in the field. Their comments are sent back to the researcher, who should address their comments and then re-submit the paper to the journal.

The purpose of this exercise is to advance the field in some way—by presenting a new analysis of another researcher's data, or by presenting new data to test theories in the field. Hence, it presents new work and is not merely a summary of other people's work.

The dissertation (for a PhD, MLitt, MPhil., MA and now the BA) is a version of the research paper.

A research paper is not a report. A report is an expository text that collates and presents information. Reviewers and dissertation supervisors frequently point out that the document is a report and not a research paper. A research paper, unlike a report, is an argumentative text in which the researcher identifies a gap in the current research and attempts to fill that gap with his/her data and analysis.

This aspect of the research paper is described in more detail in the Introduction, but it is the heart of the research paper. It helps you understand why the research paper is an argument and not merely an expository essay, the importance of a theoretical framework, the purpose of the literature review, and why you collect and analyse data.

Research papers have the following features.

- They are the culmination of a lot of reading, and most often data collection and analysis.
- They have a conceptual or theoretical framework that places the work within an established field.
- They present a new idea and are not merely an extension to 'the Indian context'.
- They are not expository texts; they are argumentative. That is, they try to persuade the reader (reviewer) in an informed and 'objective' fashion.

What Can Go Wrong?

If you submit your article to a paid journal, it will get accepted. This is a good start for beginning researchers who want to show a list of publications for promotion. However, at some point you might want to publish in referred journals either in India or abroad, where the standards are very high.

What can go wrong and what does one need to do? Some journal reviewers merely write back, 'Get an editor', which is one way of saying that the paper does not follow accepted conventions. Other reviewers point to specific problems, some of which I have given below, organised by their frequency; these problems have become so common that numerous articles have begun to appear on websites that point out basic errors in writing up a research paper for publication.

The author has not followed the instructions

Each journal has its own conventions that are given in a document called *Instructions to Authors.* Even before writing the paper, we usually identify a few journals and then write the paper to suit the audience and conventions of each journal.

However, a common mistake is to write a paper and then submit it to a journal without looking at sample papers in the journal or reading the *Instructions to the Author.* If writers took the time to look at other papers in the journal, they would realise that the Introduction normally does not include figures, which their paper has done. If writers read the *Instructions to the Author,* they would realise that the journal allows 500 words (2 pages) for a book review, whereas they have written a 20-page review.

The paper has no data

Without data, the paper is merely an opinion piece that belongs in a blog or on Facebook. Data is at the heart of papers in the sciences and social sciences, but even literature and history include an analysis of primary texts or secondary documents; without this evidence, the researcher's opinion comes across as grand statements that are easily dismissed or demolished.

The paper has no conceptual or theoretical framework

You think your data is fascinating, but your analysis will depend on the theoretical framework or lens through which you view it. For instance, if I have collected classroom data on how Indian school children learn to read and write in English, I can frame the study in different ways—as a study of emergent literacy, as a critique of teaching methods, to explain how school children learn to memorise, to describe the development of second language acquisition etc. For each paper, the theoretical framework, literature review and analysis would be different, and I would submit each paper to a journal that specialises in that small area.

Novice writers think that a literature review can take the place of a theoretical framework, which becomes a problem in the social sciences where there are multiple ways of analysing the same data depending on the theoretical framework. This is reflected in the fact that there are hundreds of journals in a discipline, each with a slightly different orientation. Rejection by a journal does not necessarily mean that your paper is bad; you may have chosen the wrong journal.

The absence of a theoretical framework may be due to the recent surge in 'paid' journals that publish any papers that are submitted, resulting in a grab bag of articles from different disciplines, such as applied linguistics, literature and language policy. Researchers get the impression that they merely need to include a few references (from different theoretical frameworks) and then say, 'in the Indian context.....'

The literature review is outdated and/or not relevant

Too many researchers think that the purpose of the literature review is 'display behaviour' to show that they have covered the important material in the discipline, and they insert long quotations from the material they have read. However, it is assumed that as a serious researcher you have read and digested the books and papers in your field; citing an undergraduate textbook such as Samuelson in an economics paper shows that you are still learning economics. And no one has time to read a history of the field; we all know it. All this is background information that readers know and assume that the researcher knows. In disciplines such as computer science, papers begin with a direct statement of the problem.
For the literature review, you have to pick from the thousands of articles that have been published in your research area. Since the purpose of the research paper is to present an argument, you should pinpoint articles that are relevant to your argument—both for and against. This requires access to the original articles in JSTOR and extensive reading; you cannot cite abstracts that you found on the Internet, because the full article may discuss caveats that are not given in the abstract.

The statistical analysis is incorrect

If you haven't done a course in statistics, please don't report statistical analyses. Social science researchers have started jazzing up their papers with numbers that they get from a statistician, but the test is often inappropriate for the data and undermines the credibility of both the researcher and the journal.

As a reviewer, I have rejected papers in which the researcher gives the mean of a Likert scale; Kostoulas (2013) says it better: calculating mean values of a Likert scale makes as much sense as suggesting that 'the average of a watermelon and two strawberries is an apple'.[1] A Mann Whitney test is used to compare two groups; you cannot use it to compare the same group on two tests. And something is clearly wrong with a t-test table that gives 5000 degrees of freedom. All this is covered in Statistics 101, which you should do before you attempt to include statistics.

The best way to go about writing a research paper is to look at similar papers in your field. Identify an article from a referred journal in your field; try to find the most important journal in your field, which is called a Tier 1 journal. If you plan to publish your paper in a specific journal, get a copy of an article from that journal. Do not use a chapter from a textbook or an article from a magazine, because those are different genres. Make a photocopy of the article. When going through this chapter, keep checking whether your photocopied article follows the conventions described. If they do not, think about why they differ. Perhaps there are different conventions in your field; computer science, for example, is such a recent field that research articles do not have established conventions.

---

[1]Kostoulas, A, (2013). Four things you probably didn't know about Likert scales. Available at https://achilleaskostoulas.com/2013/09/09/four-things-you-probably-didnt-know-about-likert-scales/. Last accessed April 4, 2017.

If you are an acknowledged expert in your field, you can do what you want and your work will still be published. However, the structure that we discuss in this chapter is becoming increasingly frozen. Both journals and readers have come to expect this structure in all research papers and you risk losing out if you deviate from it.

In the following sections, we deal with the structure of a research paper and each section, highlighting the kind of language that is used and the conventions followed. It is based on linguistic studies of the structure and language of texts, where they found remarkable similarity across disciplines and journals. There is some variation among disciplines and journals, so you should check with the journal requirements.

Sections of a Research Paper

Figure 11.1 shows the sections of a research paper, thesis, or dissertation. The shaded sections are the core sections, and the other sections may be included. The shaded sections would be divided further depending on your discipline; here we have shown the format for a typical paper in the social sciences, such as psychology, but in your discipline, you may not need to collect primary data, in which case you would have different sections. For a dissertation, you need to include a Table of Contents at the beginning, as well as a list of figures and tables.

For now, note the following in Figure 11.1.

1. The order of the sections—what comes first, what next, etc.
2. The shape of the section. Some sections are not rectangular blocks; the Introduction and Conclusion are funnel-shaped, with one part wider than the other.

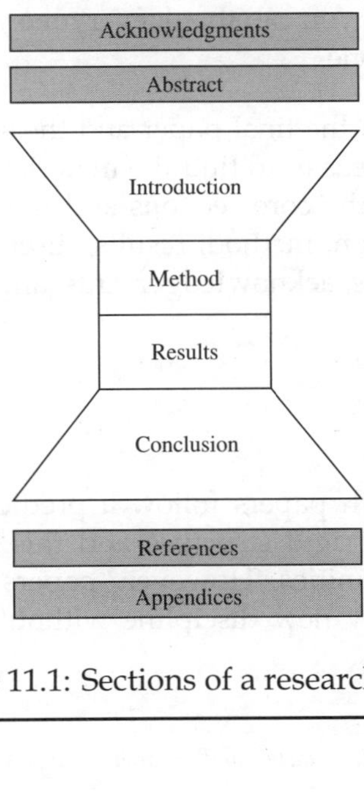

Figure 11.1: Sections of a research paper

Sequence of Writing

Although the completed research paper follows the structure shown in Figure 11.1, the sections are not written in this sequence. The Introduction is the most difficult section to write. Many writers get stuck at the Introduction and cannot move forward. Also, if you begin with the Introduction, you reach the Conclusion only to find that you have to re-write the Introduction and maybe even other sections of the paper. Experienced writers do the Introduction *last*. At this point you know what you want to say and can frame the Introduction clearly.

Here is a sequence that works well. Begin with what you already have and is the core of your paper; then add the other sections and revise the entire paper so that you have a consistent 'story'.

Suggested sequence for writing

1. **Method.** Write down how you collected the data.
2. **Results.** What are the results of the analysis?
3. **Discussion and Conclusion.** What does your data tell you? What are the implications?
4. **Introduction.** Frame your research for the audience.
5. **References.** Match references to work cited in the sections above, especially the Introduction.
6. **Abstract.** Create the abstract using sentences from different sections of the paper.
7. **Acknowledgements.** Now you can thank everyone who helped because the paper is done.

Since the sequence of sections in the final paper and the sequence of writing the paper is conflicting in nature, to make it easier to find the material you need, I have organised the rest of this chapter in terms of the core sections and the peripheral sections. While the former comprises the introduction, method, results, discussion and conclusion, the latter comprises the abstract, references, acknowledgements, and appendices.

The Core Sections

Studies have found that research papers follow a predictable structure (Swales 1990)[2]. Papers in the sciences follow a rigid structure and this is now emulated in the social sciences and even in the humanities. However, papers in computer science are free flowing, since this is a relatively new discipline without a long tradition of published research.

[2]Swales, J. (1990). *Genre analysis: English in academic and research settings.* Cambridge University Press.

The introduction

The Introduction should make up only 10% of your paper.

Purpose of the introduction

The Introduction provides a context for the paper. It does this by (a) mentioning the topic through keywords, (b) highlighting the importance of this topic, and (c) placing the paper within a research space. The second half of the Introduction narrows down to focus on the paper: it defines the scope of the paper, ending with a thesis statement, and in the case of a long paper, it describes the main sections of the paper. Figure 11.2 depicts this narrowing from the general to the specific in introductions.

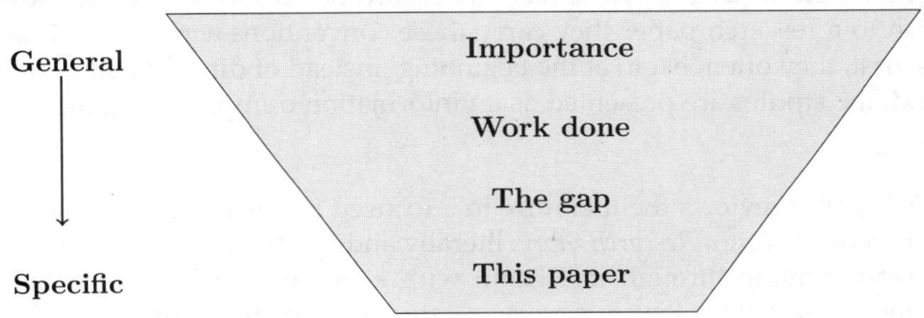

Figure 11.2: Introduction of a research paper

Sections of the introduction

The Introduction is organised into four Moves (Swales 1990).

Move 1. Importance of the topic

The Introduction (and the paper) begins by indicating that the topic is important. In the examples below, words indicating the topic and importance have been given in *italics*.

Examples

- In today's global economy, accuracy in predicting trends of foreign exchange rates is *crucial* for future investment.
- *Sensors* are *essential* in the fields of science, engineering, and medicine. Moreover, there is a *demand* for *software systems* that effectively use the data measured by these sensors.
- *Multi-agent systems* are *important* for representing and analysing complex systems.

Papers in computer science usually identify and describe a problem in this move.

- Consumers depend on online reviews to purchase products and to book services, but many of these reviews are fake or misleading.

Move 2. Work done

This move describes relevant research that has already been done and its purpose is to advance your argument. For this, you carefully select critical papers in the field and when describing these studies, you extract only those points that are pertinent to your argument.

In a dissertation, this move warrants a separate chapter called *Literature Review.* It demonstrates your scholarship—that you have read and understood the vast literature in the field. Feak and Swales (2009)[3] provide strategies such as mind maps for organising the voluminous literature, which is helpful for PhD students who must write a chapter called *Literature Review.*

However, in a research paper this section is much shorter; it forms part of the introduction and is not marked off as a separate section. Unfortunately, when writers move from the dissertation to a research paper they carry these conventions across, which leads to two problems: first, they often 'begin at the beginning' instead of directly addressing the topic, and second, the studies are presented as an information dump, leaving the reader to ask, 'So what?'

The research paper reviews the literature in a focused manner. I take the title of the Feak and Swales book, *Telling a Research Story,* literally and so I structure this section as a 'story' with a thread running through it. I begin with a seminal paper (which links it to the previous move) and then I weave relevant studies into my argument. These studies address questions that the topic would raise; some are merely lists for coverage, but studies that impact your argument or analysis are described in greater detail.

- *Beginning with a seminal paper. (The topic is the use of PowerPoint.)*

  The second feature of such programs is their structure, namely, the physical layout of the slides or the 'real estate'. This has come in for some extremely sharp criticism by Tufte (2003). He argues that the landscape format of the slides (versus the portrait orientation of an A4 page) along with the use of bullet points and large fonts (for easy viewing) forces the author to condense the information, often omitting information that is critical but does not fit onto one slide; in fact, he attributes the accident to the Columbia space shuttle in 2003 to the omission of crucial information in a PowerPoint presentation (cf. Dumont 2005 Shwom and Keller 2003).

- *Coverage organised alphabetically by country*

  Several studies have documented the use of English in bilingual advertisements in different countries — in Ecuador (Alm 2003), France and Germany (Hilgendorf and Martin 2001; Martin 2002a, 2002b Piller 2001), Ireland (Kelly-Holmes 2005), Japan (Takashi 1990a, 1990b, 1992 Wilkerson 1997), Korea (Jung 2001 Lee 2006), Mexico (Baumgardner 2006), and Russia (Ustinova 2006 Ustinova and Bhatia 2005).

[3]Feak, C.B. & Swales, J.M. (2009). *Telling a research story: Writing a literature review.* University of Michigan Press.

- *The argument (and not the study) takes precedence*

    Surveys in a related field (namely, SMEs and technical writers) found that SMEs have scant respect for the skills of the technical writers they deal with (Walkowski 1991) and are often hostile because of fear of losing the job (Yancy 1995). At the same time, technical writers complain about the lack of accessibility to the SME and the SME's lack of respect for the writer's work (Lee and Mehlenbacher 2000).

- *Describing a study that supports your argument*

    Although this diversity can generate innovative solutions through synergy, problems arise when the differences are very great. Guri-Rosenblit (2003) points out that these collaborative ventures in eLearning have often failed and attributes their failure to the enormous difference between 'the organizational cultures of these two worlds' (p. 15); where corporations expect decisions to be made fast and deadlines to be met, academics spend large amounts of time on reflection and deliberation.

- *Be kind (I disagree with the highly influential work of Gelb, but offer a recent alternative.)*

    One typology of writing systems is given in Gelb (1952). Since Gelb's focus was the evolution of writing systems from the logography through the syllabary to the alphabet, writing systems such as the Indic scripts and the Semitic scripts fell somewhere between the three and were given differing labels, usually hyphenated; Indic scripts have been termed 'quasi-syllabaries' (Gelb 1952 Justeson and Stephens 1994), while Hebrew and Arabic have been called 'consonantal syllabaries' (Gelb 1952). To place all writing systems at the same level, Daniels (1992, 1996) uses the terms *abugida* and *abjad* for the Indic and Semitic writing systems, respectively.

By the end of the literature review, it should become clear that certain questions or aspects are important but missing. This allows the argument to flow into Move 3.

Move 3. The gap

Move 3 identifies a gap in the research area that your paper will fill. It is a critical component of a research paper, but is often skipped by novice writers. This move enables a transition from the literature review to the work in your study.

The gap is signalled by words such as *however, although* and *nevertheless.*

Examples

- **Although** historical data is a major factor in the prediction process, we do not know whether they are effective.
- **Nevertheless,** few studies have examined the impact of.....

To understand why this move is important, compare a research paper to a report. Reports do not identify a gap in the research literature; they merely collate relevant information for the reader and are expository texts. A research paper, on the other hand, is an argumentative/persuasive text; your argument depends on this 'turn' from what has been done to what you will do.

Journal reviewers and dissertation supervisors frequently point to the absence of this move in their comments. Often, there is a literature review in Move 2 with a jump to Move 4, so the purpose of the literature review is not clear and the reader is left asking, 'So what?'

Move 4. What this paper does

In this move, you state how your paper contributes to the field and your specific research question. It may even summarise the findings as below.

> **Example**
> This paper examines the beliefs that pre-service teachers held about the teaching of reading—their entering beliefs, which aspects of the training were the most easily accepted, and how they tried to reconcile instruction with their existing belief systems. It found that trainees most readily accepted changes when they could relate them to a gap in their school education; other instruction only marginally affected them during the short course.

Move 5. Other structure of the paper

This section is optional. It is used when the paper is longer than 20 pages.

> The paper is organised as follows. First, we describe....

Method and analysis

Without evidence, your research paper is merely an opinion piece. It must be supported with evidence—data that you collected, data or texts that you analysed etc. In this section, you describe how you selected or collected data and your method of analysis. In this section, you should provide sufficient detail about your project for two reasons. First, if there is insufficient information, it gives the impression that your findings are not sound and, second, other researchers may want to extend your project and need sufficient detail to replicate the study.

For data collection and analysis, we rely on what we learn in courses about research methods, either quantitative or qualitative.

Types of data

There are two types of data.

- *Primary data* is what you collect. You might interview people, conduct surveys, observe classes, conduct an experiment, etc.

- *Secondary data* is what is published by other researchers. Huge datasets, such as the Census of India, are available, which researchers can use for different types of analyses.

In terms of research, data gathering takes up the maximum time. Every researcher struggles to gain access to schools or organisations, to obtain databases that are either not available or outrageously expensive, or to chase responses to surveys. All this is an inescapable part of doing research and does not need to be recorded in the research paper.

Confidentiality

If you are working with human beings (as in interviews, psychological tests, etc.), you need to protect the identity of your subjects. The reason is that your analysis could show them in a bad light that might later be used against them by supervisors, teachers, etc.

The rules for confidentiality are extremely strict in Western countries. In the U S, the researcher must get clearance and permission for the project from a committee, each subject must sign a consent form, and the data must be securely locked. Since these practices are not followed in India, it has adversely affected business dealings with the European Union and the US who cannot trust data confidentiality in India.

What does this mean for the researcher? At a minimum, do the following.

- **Step 1.** Create a consent form and ask each subject to sign one (see Appendix A). Then, keep these in a safe place.
- **Step 2.** In your write-up, make sure that subjects cannot be identified. This means you cannot use their photographs, business designations, or real names; you can use pseudonyms but make sure that these match their gender and ethnicity.

Example
All participant names are pseudonyms. Pseudonyms reflect the ethnic identity and language background of the participant.

Describing the method

Here you describe the participants (who), materials (what), and procedure (how).

- *Participants.* Describe the number of participants and their background. You may have to describe how they were selected—the sampling frame, whether the subjects were paid or were volunteers, etc. If you have an experimental design, describe how the groups were set up. Also, the identity of the participants must be concealed. (See the section on confidentiality above.)
- *Materials.* The materials could be a questionnaire, experimental stimuli, etc. Describe the material in brief; if it is fascinating or relevant, include the material in an appendix after the paper.
- *Procedure.* Describe what the participants did. Write this as a walkthrough, so that readers can visualise step-by-step what participants did.

You should provide sufficient detail to allow other researchers to replicate your study. However, do not burden the reader with your research problems, because we've all been there.

Describing the analysis

In the analysis, you describe the tools and your procedure to analyse the data.

In selecting the tools and cleaning up the data, you make choices. Which statistical package should I use? Which is more appropriate—t-tests or an ANOVA? Which data points should I drop? If you are using the standard method in the field, you can merely report your decisions. However, if the tools or procedure are new or controversial, you need to discuss the alternatives and justify your choice.

The analysis can be complicated or dense, so help the reader understand. To help the reader, explain why you used a specific procedure.

> **Example**
> To reduce the number of variables, a one-way ANOVA was conducted, using Commercial textbooks and Government textbooks as the two factors. Fifteen indices were found to be significant ($p<0.05$).

In terms of language, most of the section is usually written in the past tense, because the data has already been collected and analysed. However, disciplines such as economics use the present tense.

> **Example**
> To identify the variables, we first **use**....

Results

This section presents the results of the data analysis. The results are not interpreted here; instead, they come under Discussion. The results are reported in the past tense.

If you have used a statistical analysis, the numbers are reported here; sometimes, computer code is included in this section. For qualitative data, the main trends are summarised with sample protocols. Since this section is dense, you can make it readable by presenting the information in a visual form. Tufte (1983, 1990)[4] is still relevant for the principles that inform data visualisation and how to display quantitative data.[5]

Researchers read this section carefully if they want to replicate the findings or critique the paper; otherwise, this section receives less attention from readers than the discussion that follows.

---

[4]Tufte, E.R. (1983). *The Visual Display of Quantitative Information*. Connecticut: Graphics Press. Tufte, E.R. (1990). *Envisioning Information*. Connecticut: Graphics Press.

[5]For advanced data display techniques, see Heer, J. Bostock, M., and Ogievetsky, V. (2010). A Tour through the Visualization Zoo. *Communications of the ACM*, 53, 6, 59-67. Available at http://hci.stanford.edu/jheer/files/zoo/.

> Note: Save the word *significant* for statistical results that report a significance level. Use a bland synonym instead.

Describing Data

Only you can understand your raw data. You need to summarise it and then present it in a form that a reader can understand. You can present your data in the form of tables, text, or figures; other data display types are images and line drawings. Since there are different conventions in each discipline, I will merely highlight a few decisions in choosing among the main options.

If you use a table or a figure, don't leave the reader to figure out how to interpret it. You should refer to the table/figure in your text and highlight the main findings.

Tables

Tables are used when precise numbers are required (such as the output of a statistical analysis).

Tables are also used to summarise qualitative data, which can be voluminous. When the data stretches to hundreds of pages, it becomes difficult to interpret and impossible to read. Resist the temptation to include all the protocols in the main text, and instead move it to an appendix. You can summarise the data in a table, which helps the reader identify the main trends at a glance. For further clarity, you can add a few pertinent quotes.

Table 11.1 Use of past tense and plurals during story recitation in Upper KG (n=13)

Words	1	2	3	4	5	6	7	8	9	10	11	12	13
Past Tense													
became	x	✓	✓			✓		✓	✓		✓	✓	✓
stuck		✓		✓		✓		✓	✓		✓	✓	✓
gathered	✓	✓		✓	✓	✓		✓	✓	✓		✓	✓
wanted		✓					✓	✓	✓		✓	✓	✓
joined	x	x		x	x			x	x		x	x	x
looked	x	x		x	x	x		x	x	✓	x	x	✓
Plurals													
crows	✓	✓			✓			✓		✓	✓	✓	✓
friends		✓			✓ x	✓		✓	✓	x✓	x	x	✓
feathers	✓	x	✓	✓	✓	✓		✓	✓	✓	✓	✓	✓
peacocks	x	✓			x			x		x	x	x	x

Note:

✓ indicates correct morpheme
x indicates missing morpheme
Blank cell indicates omitted word

Text

If the numbers are simple, they can be reported as part of the text.

> **Examples**
> The results show that text length was significant ($p<0.004$). The NCERT textbook has the shortest texts (range 131–457 words), whereas the commercial books show a steady increase, so that by Grade 4 they reach 687 words (Textbook 1), 836 words (Textbook 2), and 1,177 words (Textbook 3).

Figures

Figures help readers visualise the data. As an alternative to the text above, we could use a figure. I have used a line diagram because I want to show a trend over time.

> Figure 1 displays the mean number of words in texts on the four textbooks from Grade 1 to Grade 4. The NCERT textbook has the shortest texts (range 131–457 words), whereas the commercial books show a steady increase, so that by Grade 4 they reach 687 words (Textbook 1), 836 words (Textbook 2), and 1,177 words (Textbook 3).

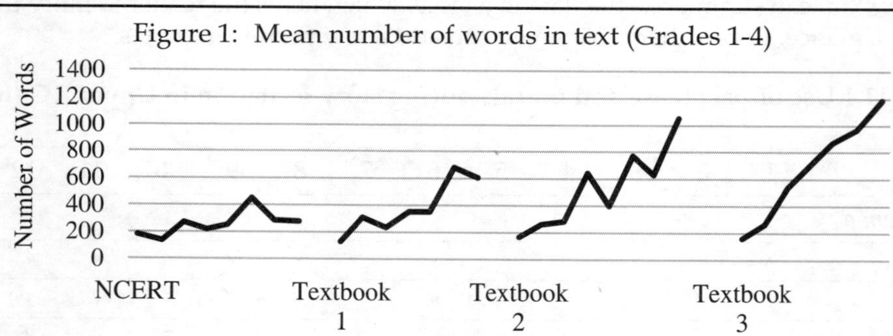

Figure 11.3: Line diagram

Complex processes are better understood through a visual. In the example below, two pages of text were packed into a single figure.

Figure 1: Sample: Pre-service teacher beliefs about reading

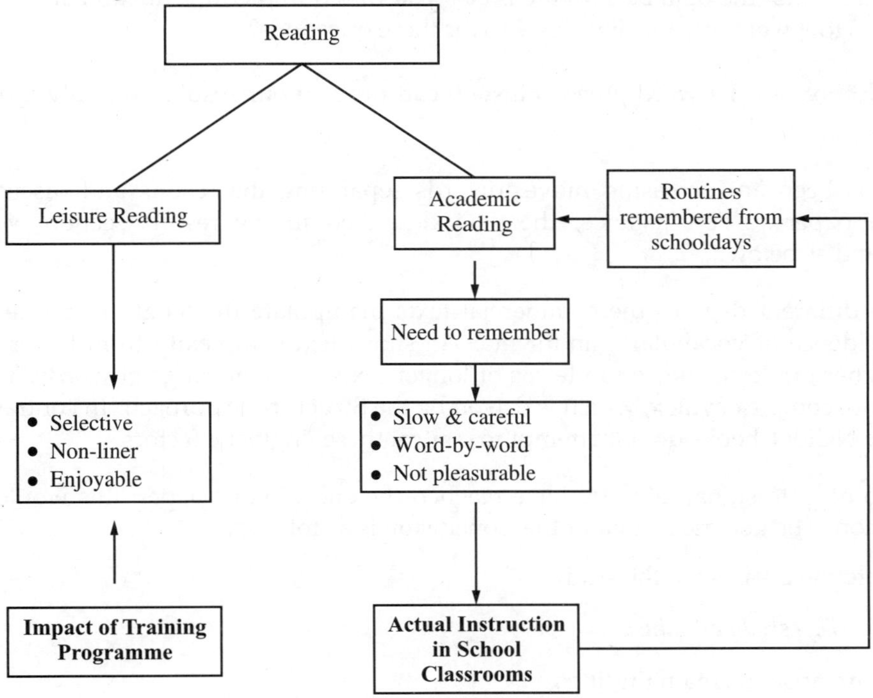

Figure 11.4: Complex process shown in a figure

Discussion and Conclusion

This section widens out and is the reverse of the introduction. It begins with a discussion of the results and then broadens to the implications for research in the area.

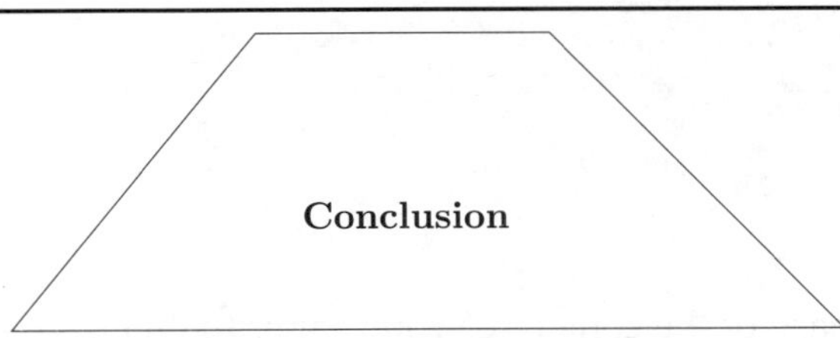

Figure 11.5: Discussion and conclusion of a research paper

In the discussion section, you provide an interpretation of your results. What does the data mean? Link the data back to the issues you raised in the Introduction and promised to cover. How well do your findings answer these questions?

Please do not use the word *prove.* Einstein can prove; your results can only indicate or suggest.

There has been an increasing move towards separating the results and discussion in research papers. For instance, the data described in the results section would be interpreted as below.

> To different degrees the commercial texts manipulate the length of the text, incidence of vocabulary, and syntax. In short, text complexity from lower to higher grades is viewed in terms of longer texts, a wider range of words, and more complex syntax, which is driven by the Structural Approach. In contrast, the NCERT books do not attempt to control these linguistic factors.

You also need to signal that you have reached the end of your paper; this would be the Conclusion. The generic format of the Conclusion is as follows.

1. State the purpose of the study.

   This study examined....

2. Summarise the main findings.

   The *results showed....*

3. Suggest future directions

   - *Further* research will examine.....
   - Two directions for *future* work are.....

The conclusion should match what was promised in the introduction, but it should not merely be a repetition of the introduction. At the same time, you cannot introduce new facts, because there should be no surprises.

Other Sections

The abstract

An abstract is a summary of the content of your paper that helps readers decide whether to read the paper. The abstract is very short—between 150 to 250 words. Some journals allow longer abstracts and these are given in the Instructions to Authors, but these rarely go over 300 words. So, be concise.

At the same time, the abstract should be complete; the reader should be able to get the gist of your paper without reading the entire paper. The reason is that the abstract is frequently available to a wide audience through journal websites or collections of abstracts; researchers skim through thousands of these abstracts, trying to decide which ones are relevant for their research. So, your abstract should allow the reader to decide whether to read your entire paper.

Elements of the abstract

Although an abstract is usually only one paragraph, the following information is packed into it.

1. *Background information.* It provides the background to the problem. This is written in the *present tense* because it is still a problem.
2. *Purpose.* Purpose of the study and the scope
3. *Method.* How you collected and analysed the data.
4. *Results.* The most important results *may* be described. Many abstracts do not give the results; for the results, you would have to get a copy of the paper.
5. Conclusion. Implications or recommendations (present tense)

Types of abstracts

Extended abstract

This is a long version of the abstract. It is usually required when you apply for a conference presentation, because it gives the committee sufficient information to decide whether your work is suitable for the conference.

Standard abstract

This is the norm for a journal article or the abstract printed for a conference.

Reduced abstract

Due to space constraints, some journals require only a reduced abstract. A reduced abstract has only the following elements: (a) Purpose + Method (b) Results (c) Conclusion, which is optional.

References

References are *not* a bibliography. A bibliography is a list of books and papers that you read or consulted; it shows the breadth of your reading and acts as a suggested list for further reading on the topic. There is no space in a journal for a bibliography.

References, on the other hand, are books and papers that you mention (or cite) in your paper. They are used to support and extend your argument, and they lend credibility to your work. Sometimes the editor returns your article with comments such as 'Reference?' or 'Can you substantiate this statement?' or even 'sweeping statement'. In such cases, it helps to cite published work that supports your point. You can see this in Wikipedia articles that are written by anonymous authors; the editor frequently adds a note that says 'citation needed'.

The material you cite could be books, journal articles, magazine articles, software programs, websites, etc. References to external sources are especially dense in sections such as the literature review. However, they also in the Method section if you discuss a procedure, in the Discussion section when you link your results to other studies, and the Conclusion if you discuss further research.

There are two parts to a citation: in-text citation and the list of references. When you mention that material in your paper, it is an in-text citation. In the reference list, you give sufficient detail about the publication so that readers can track it down.

Disciplines and journals have their own method of citing material and organising the reference list. For instance, in the social sciences, author names are given in the text, but in computer science they are merely numbered to save space (as in a Wikipedia article).

To find out how to cite material, you should consult the style guide in your discipline. You should buy a copy of the style guide, because you will need to consult it frequently.

The most common styles are—

- American Psychological Association (APA) for papers in the social sciences.
- Institute of Electrical and Electronics Engineers (IEEE) for computer science and engineering.
- Modern Language Association (MLA) for papers in the humanities.

However, disciplines may follow a modified version of these styles. For instance, economics seems to follow a modified version of the APA style.

In addition, a journal may decide to use a 'house style', which it describes in its Instructions to Authors. Since these guidelines are not comprehensive, it is best to use a sample article and format your references along the same lines.

This chapter cannot hope to cover all aspects and types of citations. Below, I have tried to describe the logic behind citations and used the APA style to show how this should be done.

In-text citations

Single authors

> Gelb (1952) proposes an evolutionary model for writing systems, but it is now accepted that there are six distinct types of writing systems (Daniels, 1996).

Multiple sources are listed alphabetically and separated by semi-colons.

> The transition into this discourse community involves learning rules of use and 'academic literacy' (Bartholomae, 1985; Johns, 1991).

A direct quotation should include the page number.

> Collaboration requires 'the coming together of diverse interests and people to achieve a common purpose via interactions, information sharing, and coordination of activities' (Jassawalla and Sashitthal, 1998; p.239).

Reference list

To help the reader locate your sources, complete information about the source is given under *References*. This allows readers to check the original source to see if your interpretation is correct or to read the original article for their own work. You should give enough information for the reader to find the source.

These are arranged alphabetically by the last name of the first author.

> Daniels, P. (1996). The world's writing systems. In P. Daniels and W. Bright (eds), *The study of writing systems*, (pp. 3–17). New York: Oxford University Press.
>
> Gelb, I. (1952). *A study of writing*. Chicago: University of Chicago Press.

If you do not have access to a library, you may not be able to read the original research paper. Some people cheat and cite the reference as if they have read the original work. The correct procedure is to give the original reference and say *cited in*.

> **Example**
> The use of a schema enables the reader to resort to 'fuzzy parsing' (Burton, 1976; cited in de Beaugrande, 1980)

Under *References*, list both sources in alphabetical order.

> Burton, R. (1976). *Semantic grammars: An engineering technique for constructing natural language understanding systems*. Cambridge, MA: Bolt, Beranek and Newman (Technical Report No. 3453).
>
> De Beaugrande, R. (1980). *Text, discourse, and process: Toward a multidisciplinary science of texts*. Norwood, NJ: Ablex Publishing Co.

Format of a reference

A reference has four major elements— author name, title of work, source, and year.

To get an idea of just how different these styles are, here is a reference written in the three different styles. APA and MLA use the author-date style, i.e., the references are arranged alphabetically; however, IEEE uses the Vancouver style in which the references are listed by the order in which they are mentioned in the text. Notice that the four elements—author name, title, source, and year—are in different positions and each style uses different punctuation marks.

APA	Twigge, A. & Wood, B. (2009). Japanese text entry on mobile phones versus computers. *Journal of Text Entry,* 4, 5, 1–19.
MLA	Twigge, Ann and Wood, Bob. "Japanese text entry on mobile phones versus computers." *Journal of Text Entry,* 4.5 (2009): 1–19.
IEEE	[1] A. Twigge and B. Wood, "Japanese text entry on mobile phones versus computers," *J. Text Entry,* vol. 4, pp. 1–19, 2009.

The following pages list how to refer to the basic types of documents in three styles—APA, MLA, and IEEE. We cover only the basics—journal articles, books, chapters in books, conference papers, etc. This is only the tip of the iceberg—there is a world of documents such as translated books, reports from private organisations, electronic versions, dissertation abstracts, online sources, multimedia, and computer software, each of which is formatted differently. For more detailed information, you will have to refer to the printed version of the style guide or find examples on the Internet. Since these manuals are not easy reading; we go back to our original suggestion—photocopy a sample article and follow the format. In fact, that's how all of us wrote our dissertations.

APA style

In the reference list, the entries are arranged alphabetically. Each entry is formatted for the following: order of initials, capital letters, use of commas and full stops, and use of italics.

The format varies depending on where the material is published—in a book, a journal, as a report, etc. Below are some of the formats you would use; for additional formats, you need to refer to the APA Style Manual.

Book

Brewe, A., Potts, B., & Tee, C. (2004). *How languages are learned: Studies in language acquisition*. Mahwah, NJ: Erlbaum.

Edited Book

Banks, B.C. (Ed.). (2002). *Dancing in the dark*. New York: Wiley.

Howe, J. & Banks, B.C. (Eds.). (1999). *Bilingualism around the world.* New York: Wiley.

Chapter in a Book

Sunne, S. (1997). Bright and early: Primary school education in the US. In T. Trighte (Ed.), *Primary schooling around the world* (pp. 158–172). London: Sage.

Article in a Journal

Patel, I. (2017). Never too late: Adult literacy in India. *Journal of Adult Education, 126,* 110–124.

Unpublished Dissertation

Rani, V.S. (1995). *A study of the composing processes of ESL learners at the secondary level*. Unpublished M.Phil. dissertation, Central Institute of English and Foreign Languages, Hyderabad, India.

Conference Proceedings
Kaplan, S.S. & Smith, C. (2013). Users who think. In G. Waas (Ed.), *Proceedings of the 24th HCI Conference*, Prague, Czech Republic.
Unpublished Conference Paper
Mettle, M.M. (2016, May). *The effects of prior instruction on student writing in Asia.* Paper presented at the International Reading Association conference, San Francisco.
Newspaper Article (with and without author)
Jenkins, S. (2009, April 3–9). Treasures belong to world, not to curators. *The Guardian Weekly, 180*, p.20. Brown retreats on spending as investors signal caution. (2009, April 3–9). *The Guardian Weekly, 180*, p.13.
Magazine Article (with and without author)
Patel, I. (2009, March). Duck! The teacher is looking at you. *Schools and Schooling, 22*, 31–32. Children on the run: Dropouts from the system. (2009, March 21–25). *Education Today, 377*, 45.
Reports and Working Papers (with and without author)
Ramesh, B. (2006). *Village development versus wildlife protection in Ranikhet* (Technical Report No. 66). New Delhi: Institute of Development. Institute of Development (2007). *The greening of Uttarakhand* (Working paper 315). New Delhi: Government of India.

Online material is referenced in the same way with one addition. Add an extra line giving the url. If the website is likely to be here today and gone tomorrow, give the date when you retrieved it.

Online article
Gupta, R. & Mehra, P. (2006). Speaking versus communicating in business English. *Language in India*, 6. Retrieved April 22, 2017.

1. Many Authors

If there are more than six authors (and in science, the number can go up to 36 authors), list only the first six and then add et al. (meaning 'the rest').

> H. Abramson, S. Bhalla, K.T. Christianson, J.M. Goodwin, J.R. Goodwin, J. Sarraille et al. (1996, June). *Multimedia, multilingual hyperdictionaries: A Japanese -English example.* Paper presented at the Joint International Conference of Association for Literary and Linguistic Computing and Association for Computers and the Humanities, Bergen, Norway.

2. Sorting the references

a. Arrange the references alphabetically, that is, **Abe, A.B.** is followed by **Ackerman, C.D.**

Alm, C. O. (2003). English in the Ecuadorian commercial context. *World Englishes, 22*, 2, 143–158.

Banu, R.& Sussex, R.(2001). Code-switching in Bangladesh. *English Today, 17*, 51–61.

b. If Bhatia has written several works, arrange them chronologically, starting with the earliest publication.

Bhatia, T. K. (1987). English in advertising: Multiple mixing and media. *World Englishes, 6*, 1, 33–48.

Bhatia, T. K. (1992). Discourse functions and pragmatics of mixing: Advertising across cultures. *World Englishes, 11*, 2/3, 195–215.

c. If Bhatia has published work alone as well as with other authors, list his solo work first.

Bhatia, T.K. (2006). World Englishes in global advertising. In B.B. Kachru, Y. Kachru, and C.L. Nelson (Eds.). *The handbook of world Englishes* (pp. 601–619). Blackwell Publishing Ltd.

Bhatia, T.K. & Ritchie, W.C. (2004). Bilingualism in the global media and advertising. In T.K. Bhatia & W.C. Ritchie (Eds.), *The handbook of bilingualism* (pp. 513–546). Blackwell Publishing Ltd.

d. If Takashi is a prolific writer and has published two or more works in the same year, your first in-text citation will be Takashi (Yeara) and the second one is Takashi (Yearb). In the references, arrange these works in the same order.

Takashi, K. (1990a). English elements in Japanese advertising. *English Today, 6*, 45–46.

Takashi, K. (1990b). A sociolinguistic analysis of English borrowings in Japanese advertising texts. *World Englishes, 9*, 327–341.

MLA style

The Modern Language Association (MLA) style is used for papers in the liberal arts and humanities. MLA style has recently changed—they have replaced underline with italics. If you use this style, make sure you refer to the latest version of the manual. Below we have a few samples from the types of sources that are frequently used in this area.

Journal article
Gilroy, Paul. "Nationalism, History, and Ethnic Absolutism." *History Workshop Journal*, 30 (1990): 114-20.
O'Hanlon, Rosalind, and David Washbrook. "After Orientalism–Culture, Criticism, and Politics in the Third World." *Comparative Studies in Society and History* 34.1 (1992): 141-67.

Book

Glass, Ruth. *Clich s of Urban Doom and Other Essays*. Oxford: Basil Blackwell, 1989.

Piore, M. J., and C.F. Sabel. *The Second Industrial Divide: Possibilities for Property*. New York: Basic Books, 1984.

Edited Book or Anthology

Guha, Ranajit, and Gayatri Chakravorty Spivak, eds. *Selected Subaltern Studies*. New York: Oxford University Press, 1988.

Work in an Anthology, Reference, or Collection

Shamir, Shimon. "West Bank Refugees—Between Camp and Society." *Palestinian Society and Politics*. Ed. Joel Migdal. Princeton, NJ: Princeton University Press, 1980. 24-34.

Unpublished Dissertation

Varma, Promodini. "The Play of Being: Kleinian Themes in the Plays of Samuel Beckett." Diss. University of Delhi, 1993.

Translated Book

Valmiki, Omprakash. *Joothan: A Dalit's Life*. Trans. Arun Prabha Mukherjee. Kolkata: Samya, 2003.

Government Publication Government of Pakistan. Ministry of Education. *Pakistan School Statistics*. Islamabad: Ministry of Education, 1993.

Poem or Short Story

Brickman, Marshall. "The Analytic Napkin." *Fierce Pyjamas: An Anthology of Humor Writing from The New Yorker*. Eds. David Remnick and Henry Finder. New York: Modern Library, 2002. 25-29.

IEEE computer society style guide

IEEE stands for the Institute of Electrical and Electronics Engineers. Their style sheet, used in computer science and engineering, is published online and frequently updated. Try the following location:

https://www.ieee.org/documents/style_manual.pdf

Here are a few samples of how the references are listed. Note that the references are not arranged alphabetically but by order of mention.

Article in a journal

G. Alvarez and P. Cavanagh, "The capacity of visual short-term memory is set both by visual information load and by number of objects," *Psychol. Sci.*, 15(2):106–111, 2004.

Article in a book

P. Kaszubski, "Enhancing a Writing Textbook: A Nationalist Perspective," *Learner English on Computer*, S. Granger, Ed., Longman, 1998, pp.172–185.

Article in conference proceedings

B. Shneiderman, "Extreme visualization: Squeezing a billion records into a million pixels," *Proc. ACM SIGMOD Int. Conf. Manag. Data*, pp. 3–12, 2008.

Book
M. Ward, G. Grinstein, and D. A. Keim, *Interactive Data Visualization: Foundations, Techniques, and Application*. A.K. Peters, 2010.
Dissertation or thesis
J. Collins, "Variations in Written English: Characterizing Authors' Rhetorical Language Choices across Corpora of Published Texts," Ph.D dissertation, Dept. English, Carnegie Mellon Univ., PA, 2003.
Technical report with report number
C. Hoffman and J. Hopcroft, Quadratic Blending Surfaces, tech. report TR-85-674, Computer Science Dept., Cornell Univ., 1985.

Appendices

Your main text should be a coherent piece of writing. However, you may have information that interrupts the flow of your argument; these include questionnaires, stimuli, participant responses, datasets, and computer code. They are invaluable for researchers who want to replicate your study. You don't have to throw them away—you can place them in an appendix or separate appendices.

Appendices are labelled with letters, e.g., Appendix A and Appendix B.

Acknowledgements

- Thank everyone who helped. If you don't, they won't help you the next time you need them.
- Use the word *thankful* with care. It means *relieved* and not *grateful*. So, we would say, 'I am *grateful* for my supervisor's support and *thankful* that the project is over.'
- Spell people's names correctly and give their correct titles and designations. What is the point of being thanked if you cannot find your name in a paper or thesis?
- Acknowledge funding sources. If you received a grant or scholarship for the research, say so. The agency will be grateful for the publicity and give you further funds; it also enhances your professional qualifications, showing that you are capable of applying for and winning competitive funds.
- In research articles, acknowledgments are very brief and matter of fact. They come as a footnote or an endnote, and acknowledge professional support and input for that specific paper.

In theses and dissertations, acknowledgments are not a footnote but a separate section and range from 250 words to 2 pages. These are not merely research documents, but a slice of a researcher's life when s/he juggled work, family, and thesis requirements (such as data collection, write-up, missing supervisors, etc.). When it is over, the relief is poured out into the acknowledgments.

Step back and be matter-of-fact. You want to convey the impression that you are a competent researcher who can do independent research in your professional career. During the writing of this thesis or paper, many people helped you; your supervisor provided guidance, because that is his or her job, and your friends and family provide emotional support. Thank them for helping you get this work done. But don't give the impression that your future research and work depends on this entourage. Too much gratitude will make you sound helpless and incapable of independent research.

EXERCISES

The Introduction

Q1. Find a research article from your field; it should be from a referred international journal. Read the introduction and check the following:

1. Does it follow the structure outlined above? If not, why?
2. What words signal the different sections?

Q2. Read the first two paragraphs of the following article and decide whether it follows the structure of an Introduction. Underline the key words/phrases for each section.

Old Beliefs Impede Training in Reading Instruction

Introduction

How do novice teachers acquire the skills and knowledge necessary for their professional careers? Teacher training programs are predicated on the notion that beginning teachers lack certain skills and knowledge that need to be taught but the research shows that beginning teachers are not completely open to such instruction. Instead, novice teachers come with prior beliefs (Anderson, 1984; Hollingsworth, 1989; Shulman, 1987) that may originate in their school days and act as filters (Calderhead & Robson, 1991; Feiman-Nemser & Buchmann, 1986; Lortie, 1975; Weinstein, 1989; Zeichner & Liston, 1987). While some beliefs may be necessary for teacher-identity, if others are not changed the cycle of traditional instruction cannot be broken.

Obviously, these beliefs are not equally rigid and some of them are more amenable to change than others. Congruence between teachers' and trainees' beliefs is one factor that affects change (Tillema, 1994). Here, we use the area of reading to identify other factors underlying trainee resistance to change. This paper examines the beliefs that pre-service teachers held about the teaching of reading—their entering beliefs, which aspects of the training were the most easily accepted and how they tried to reconcile instruction with their existing belief systems. It found that trainees most readily accepted changes when they could relate them to a gap in their own training during their student days; other instruction only marginally affected them in the short duration of the course.

The Abstract

Create reduced abstracts for the texts below. For the first abstract, the answer is given.

Text 1

Bilingual and Biscriptal Slogans: English Language Advertisements in India

Abstract

Bilingual advertisements are a site of language contact (Piller, 2003), providing insights into how language is used in society. In the past 20 years, there has been an increased use of code-mixing in advertisements in countries in Asia (Banu& Sussex, 2001; Bhatia, 1992) as well as Europe (Piller, 2001). These studies examine the insertion of English words in local advertisements and their rationale, such as the desire to sound modern or foreign.

This paper examines recent trends in English advertisements in India; the matrix language of the slogans is an Indian language, such as Hindi, with English words inserted in the matrix. A second feature of these advertisements is that the slogans are not written in Indic scripts, such as Devanagiri, but in the Roman script, and occasionally in two different scripts. A sample slogan is "Hungry kya?" (Are you hungry?") where two languages (Hindi and English) have been mixed in a single slogan; other slogans combine two scripts (Roman and Devanagiri) in one slogan. This trend is seen in advertisements for Fast Moving Consumers Goods (FMCGs) as well as government organisations and small businesses.

The paper presents examples of bilingual/biscriptal advertisements in Delhi and examines the reasons underlying this phenomenon, namely, the multilingual population, code-switching among urban youth, and technological hurdles in using the Indic scripts.

References

Bhatia, T. K. (1992). Discourse functions and pragmatics of mixing: Advertising across cultures. *World Englishes*, 11, 2/3, 195–215.

Banu, R. & Sussex, R. (2001).Code-switching in Bangladesh. *English Today*, 17: 51–61.

Piller, I. (2001).Identity construction in multilingual advertising. *Language in Society*, 30, 153–86.

Piller, I. (2003).Advertising as a Site of Language Contact. *Annual Review of Applied Linguistics*, 23: 170–183

Answer

With the growth of globalised markets, there has been a concomitant increase in the use of bilingual advertising. Although several studies have examined the use of English in bilingual advertising in countries within the Expanding Circle, there has been less documentation of bilingual advertisements in countries in the Outer Circle, where English co-exists with other languages. This paper describes English advertisements in India, where bilingual advertising has emerged as a marketing strategy. It examines two features of the advertising slogans, namely, the use of code-mixing and the use of the Roman script, and argues that these features reflect the linguistic practices of the multilingual population in urban centers, such as Delhi.

Text 2

Learning from Our Students: Technology in the ESP Classroom

Abstract

With the expanding role of computers, educational institutions are looking at ways to incorporate technology in classrooms either through Computer-Assisted Language Learning (CALL) or Network-Based Language Teaching (NBLT). This creates an unusual problem—students are more familiar with the technology than their language teachers. Fear of appearing incompetent in front of their students drives many teachers away from experimenting with the technology and using it in their classrooms. In addition, language teachers are often unsure how the technology can be used to meet their educational objectives.

This paper describes student assignments in two English courses at a bilingual Japanese university where students major in computer science. The courses are designed to integrate students' computer expertise with language learning activities. Since the students work on UNIX, where the language teachers have limited expertise, the assignments ask students to explain specific concepts or procedures in their assignments. The benefits are discussed in terms of: (a) meeting language learning objectives (b) the authenticity of the assignments (c) student motivation, and (d) learning for the teacher.

Text 3

When Worlds Collide: Writing Instruction in Singapore

Abstract

Students entering the university face problems in writing because the university is a discourse community with its own writing conventions; for students, the transition into this discourse community involves learning rules of use and 'academic literacy' (Bartholomae, 1985; Johns, 1991). Studies show that prior experiences with writing exert a powerful influence on how students perceive writing and their role as writers. Canagarajah (2002) and Fox (1994) report on ESL students in US universities who resisted academic writing because they considered themselves accomplished writers in their earlier writing environments.

The transition to the university can be equally difficult for students in Asian countries but this transition has not been documented. This paper examines how writing is taught in Singapore and how it complicates the transition to the university for students. At the university, professors expect students to adopt a stance in their term papers and defend their position; instead, students view the task as one of knowledge display and avoid a direct statement of their opinion. Students acquire these writing conventions at the Junior College during their preparation for the General paper in the GCE 'A' Level examination where they are encouraged to write on general topics for an undefined audience; students carry these notions about writing into the university setting.

The study is based on faculty feedback, student assignments at the university, and analyses of the syllabus and examination requirements at the Junior College. The paper ends with suggestions for ways to help student writers negotiate the transition between the two discourse communities.

References

1. You have written a paper and included references. The journal wants you to follow the APA style sheet. Convert the references below to APA style.
   1. H. Abramson, S. Bhalla, K.T. Christianson, J.M. Goodwin, J.R. Goodwin, J.Sarraille (1995): Towards CD-ROM based Japanese $ English dictionaries: Justification and some implementation issues. In: Proc. 3rd Natural Language Processing Paci_c-Rim Symp. (Dec. 46, 1995), Seoul, Korea
   2. A.V. Aho, B.W. Kernighan, P.J. Weinberger (1988): The AWK programming language. Addison-Wesley, Reading
   3. A. Fox (1995): Linguistic Reconstruction: An Introduction to Theory and Method. Oxford Univ. Press, Oxford
   4. M. Hoey (1991): Patterns of lexis in text. Oxford Univ. Press, Oxford
   5. P. Kaszubski (1998): Enhancing a writing textbook: a nationalist perspective. In: S. Granger (ed.), Learner English on Computer, Longman, London
   6. G. Kennedy (1991): Between and through: The company they keep and the functions they serve. In: K. Aijmer, B. Altenberg (eds.), English corpus linguistics, Longman, New York

2. These references are for a paper on economics. How would you format them using APA style?

   Maurice Obstfeld (1996), Models of Currency Crises with Self Fulfilling Features, European Economic Review, 40, 1037–47

   Michael Bordo, Barry Eichengreen, Daniela Klingebiel and Maria Soledad Martinez Peria (2001, 'Is the Crisis Problem Growing More Severe?' Economic Policy 16 (32), April 53–82.

   Franklin Allen and Douglas Gale (1998), 'Optimal financial crises', Journal of Finance, American Finance Association, vol. 53(4), pages 1245–1284.

   ______(2000), 'Bubbles and Crises', Economic Journal, January.

   ______(2000), 'Financial Contagion', Journal of Political Economy, 108, February.

   -----------(2004), 'Financial Intermediaries and Market', Econometrica, 72 (4), July.

APPENDICES

Appendix A. Sample Consent Form

Consent Form

I am conducting a research study on (*name of study*). (*Give brief description of study in layperson's language.*)

I request your permission to use your responses/texts/data in my research. Your name and designation will not be used in the study. The data will be kept in a locked office and not be made available to other people.

....

Consent of the Subject

I understand that my responses will be used in the above research study. I have no objections to my responses and data being used for the study.

....

Signature of subject Date

Appendix B. Method

Note the level of detail that allows other researchers to replicate or evaluate the procedure. Also note what has not been reported: (a) The researchers spent six months gaining access to the school; (b) the OCR software was inadequate for the analysis, and (c) gaining access to the UNIX operating system required special permission and considerable persuasion.

Participants: Number and background. Duration	The participants were **16 students** in the **ninth grade**, who were observed over a period of **two months**. In their English classes, they wrote compositions for 60 minutes, based on visuals provided by the teacher; there was no overt language instruction because the teacher wanted students to generate text. For the first month students wrote compositions by hand. In the second month, the teacher moved the venue of the English class to the computer lab and students composed their essays directly on individual computers, using Microsoft Word Version 2.0.
Data selection. Deleted data	The handwritten compositions were transcribed and a subset of **20 essays (10 handwritten and 10 on the computer)** for each student was chosen for analysis. Four students **were dropped** from this analysis because they were often absent and did not produce the number of texts required.
Tools for analysis. Purpose of tools. Data preparation	The ***Spell*** **and** ***Word count*** **programs on UNIX were used to obtain the number of spelling errors and number of words per text**. Several spelling errors flagged by the program had to be **deleted** because, as Dobrin (1990) points out, the spelling checker flags words that are incorrectly spaced and British spellings. To correct for differences in the length of texts, the **percentage** of spelling errors per text was calculated.

Appendix C. Discussion

The text below has been taken from the Discussion section of a research paper.

Sum up results. Suggest explanations. Link to other studies	The **results show** that when students with inadequate language proficiency compose their essays on the computer, they use the spelling checker for two purposes. Like more experienced writers, they use it to locate typographical errors but they do not always act on the feedback. One reason could be the difficulty involved in coordinating multiple skills but it could also be that their attention is diverted to a second function, i.e., from word correction to word generation. This may explain why studies (such as Owston, Murphy and Wideman, 1992; Poulsen, 1991) find that student writers do not always use the suggestions offered by the spelling checker.
Further summary	Not all students use the spelling checker in these ways. Two students in the same classroom approached the spelling checker in very different ways, depending on their initial ability in writing. Students like Wang who initially produced sufficient text and for whom spelling accuracy was not a problem showed little change in their vocabulary. The spelling checker makes a difference to students like Reza who generate little text when writing by hand but recognise the potential of the spelling checker as a database that they cleverly exploit; with such students, the effects are seen in the range of vocabulary as well as a spread to the levels of syntax.

Appendix D. Conclusion

The text below is from the Conclusion section of a research paper.

Background to study. Purpose of the study. Summary of main findings	In the traditional method, Indic scripts are taught in a formal sequence that is based on sound similarity, but new approaches are being designed to make initial literacy easier for learners. **This paper described** the shape similarity method in its application to teaching Devanagari and Tamil. While the shape similarity method remains experimental in the teaching of Devanagari, it has been formalised in the teaching of Tamil in Singapore.
Description of the appraoch. Description of method	In the shape similarity method, the script symbols are not taught in their canonical phonological order but in clusters based on their visual similarity. The rationale is based on pattern perception, and assumes that it is easier to learn symbols that are visually similar and use similar strokes in writing. This would be analogous to teaching the letters *p, b, d, q,* and *g* as a cluster.
Limitations of the study. Value of approach	Without any comparative studies, it is difficult to assess whether shape similarity aids learning. However, these innovations represent efforts to move beyond the standard linguistic approach to address literacy issues from the perspective of the learner.
Limitations of the paper. Further research	This paper focused on the first stage of learning an Indic script, namely, letter recognition. Clearly there is more to learning an Indic script, such as creating Consonant+ Consonant combinations, not to mention decoding and comprehension. Yet, as the first step toward learning an Indic script, symbol discrimination is important. What is lacking is systematic research that examines and documents the effectiveness of different approaches. With such data, teaching initial literacy in an Indic script could be made more effective for learners.

Appendix E. Abstracts

Below are three versions of an abstract for a paper titled 'Working with Academic Subject Matter Experts (SMEs) for e-Learning Courses'.

Extended abstract

Background. Present tense	As universities increasingly put their courses online, some faculty members have turned to e-Learning companies to create multimedia versions of their courses; at the same time, e-Learning companies are asking university faculty to provide content for commercial versions of academic courses. The interaction between the company and the faculty member is often difficult because the two parties work on different assumptions; the e-Learning company, which is used to dealing with corporate clients, uses processes that are suitable for a Subject Matter Expert (SME) from the corporate sector. For their part, faculty members assume that their job is over when they hand the courseware over to the company and are unaware of the design team's constraints and concerns.
Purpose. Method. Past tense	This paper examines the interaction between the design team and academic SMEs to better understand how an e-Learning company can work with academic faculty when designing academic courses. The data come from three e-Learning companies based in Singapore that were working with faculty members at different international business schools. Interviews were conducted with members of one design team (project managers and instructional designers) about the problems they faced in working with both non-academic and academic SMEs; this allows one to separate the problems specific to academic SMEs. At a second site, the interaction between the academic SME, design team, and the project management team via a conference call was observed; this is supplemented with follow-up email between the academic SME and the design team. The final set of data comes from the author's interaction with two academic SMEs when designing academic e-Learning courses.
Results and discussion	The data is discussed in terms of three problems that surface when an instructional design team works with academic SMEs: • **Ownership of the course**. Non-academic SMEs are usually part of a team that develops content for training. The academic SME feels strong ownership of the content.

	• **Use of multiple modalities**. University faculty are used to reading/writing long texts, and their courses tend to be text-heavy courses that may not be suitable for on-screen reading and learning. Often, the design team needs to 'educate' the SME about alternate media, such as graphics, animation, and sound. At the same time, faculty members who understand the potential of the media are unable to convince instructional designers who operate within a strict design paradigm and project schedules.
	• **Pedagogical knowledge.** Instructional designers create courses based on learning objectives and explicit content so that the material is self-instructional. Although academics are usually not so explicit in their teaching, they possess tacit knowledge of the subject that the course designer needs to tap.
Conclusion and implications. Present tense	University faculty, once they understand the potential of multimedia, can take greater control of how their courses are designed. And since e-Learning companies are increasingly trying to work with academic SMEs, they need to adapt their processes to work smoothly with academic SMEs.

Standard abstract

Background. Purpose. Method. Results. Conclusion	As universities move toward online courses, some faculty members have turned to professional e-Learning companies for help in designing their courses; at the same time, e-Learning companies are asking university faculty to provide content for commercial versions of academic courses. This paper examines the problems when the design team at the e-Learning company works with academic Subject Matter Experts (SMEs) to create online multimedia courses. The data are drawn from interviews with instructional designers at three e-Learning companies based in Singapore, the interaction between academic SMEs and the development team via conference call, and the author's interactions with two academic SMEs. The paper focuses on three aspects of the interaction: (a) ownership of the course, (b) the use of multiple modalities, and (c) pedagogical knowledge, and discusses implications for both academic SMEs and e-Learning companies when they collaborate on projects.

Reduced abstract

Purpose. Method. Results	This paper examines the problems when the design team at the e-Learning company works with academic Subject Matter Experts (SMEs) to create online multimedia courses. The data are drawn from interviews with instructional designers at three e-Learning companies, SME interaction with the development team, and the author's interactions with two academic SMEs. The paper focuses on three aspects of the interaction: (a) ownership of the course, (b) use of multiple modalities, and (c) pedagogical knowledge.

Appendix F. Acknowledgements

- The data were collected as part of a project funded by Nanyang Technological University, Singapore. The other members of the research team were Robert Hvitfeldt and Vanithamani Saravanan.
- A version of this paper was presented at the 16th National Conference of the Japanese Association for Asian Englishes (JAFAE) held at Miyazaki, Japan in December 2004. I would like to thank Martha Clark Cummings for her comments on previous drafts.
- The parts of this section concerning the Russian and Czech languages were written based on the kind comments provided by Associate Professor Vitaly Klyuev (University of Aizu, Japan) and Associate Professor Vladislav Kubon (Charles University, Prague), respectively. We are grateful for their help.

CHAPTER 12 Presenting Your Ideas

INTRODUCTION

Presentations have become an integral part of professional life. Academics present research papers at conferences; in business organisations, people present their proposals and reports within the organisation or to clients; and government officials present their recommendations to their supervisors or the public. Even consultants have to present their work to the organisation if they want to get paid. Since presentations have become such an important part of the workplace, universities and even schools have begun preparing students by showing them how to plan and present their work to an audience.

Practical work
This chapter will make more sense if you create a presentation and work on it side-by-side. Select one of the topics below or choose a simple topic. Create a 5-minute presentation that uses 6 slides.[1]

Topics

- Solving the litter problem on campus
- The benefits of recycling
- How to evaluate a website

Purpose of a Presentation

An oral presentation may appear to be unnecessary duplication. After all, you have written a dissertation or a research paper, a memo or a report. People can read your document. Why do they ask you to talk about it? There are four situations in which why you may be called on to present your work.

First, it establishes your credibility. The *viva voce* for a PhD degree fulfils this function and ensures that you are the actual author of the dissertation. Second, it gives authors a forum

[1]Note to the Teacher. To increase student participation, you can assign different students the task of moderating the discussion, asking questions, and rating the presentation. A sample feedback sheet is given in the Appendix at the end of this chapter.

where they can get feedback. This happens in conferences where researchers present work in progress; based on feedback from the audience, they revise the paper and publish it in a journal. Third, oral presentations are an effective way to disseminate information; it is a 20-minute summary for busy people. Finally, and this is crucial in business organisations where time is important, the group can make an immediate decision after an oral presentation.

Components of a Presentation

There are three primary parts in an oral presentation.

1. The *speech* is the most important. The average time for a presentation is 15–20 minutes, because the attention span of the audience dwindles after 15 minutes. However, the length of the presentation depends on the situation.

   Whatever the time limit, it is a limit; the audience gets restless if you go over the time limit and moderators may cut you off.

   Fifteen minutes sounds like a lot of time, but if you have something important to say, you will find that it goes very fast. Hence, you need to plan (and maybe even rehearse) your speech to make sure that you do not go over the time limit.

   By convention, you speak uninterrupted during your presentation. Listeners have to save their comments and questions for the question and answer session that follows.

2. *Question and Answer Session (Q&A).* After you finish speaking, the audience can ask questions. This is the difficult part, because you have to listen carefully and answer to the point.

   The amount of time varies; in a conference, five minutes is the norm because this allows the audience to ask you to clarify or explain specific points you have made; if people are interested in further details, they speak with you after you have left the podium. In situations where a decision has to be made, this session lasts much longer so that the group can discuss critical points.

   What is the purpose of the Q&A? In a dissertation *viva voce,* the Q&A is an opportunity for professors to test the candidate's understanding of the content. In other situations the presentation is really like a classroom lecture; the audience listens and tries to gain knowledge for their own purposes. However, many people misunderstand the purpose of the Q&A. People in the audience sometimes think that this is an opportunity for them to give a speech. Or they treat it as a confrontation and attack the presenter. The role of the moderator is crucial here in making sure that the presenter is not bullied and that the discussion remains on track; s/he has to step in and firmly cut off the questioner. See the section below on handling the Q&A session.

3. *Handouts.* Some presenters like to prepare handouts for the audience. Handouts have several advantages. Some people are more visual and prefer reading to listening. Those who missed your talk can get a version through the handout and it is good reference material for people who attended your talk. In a small group that has to arrive at a decision, handouts make sure that everyone can refer to a document for the discussion.

   Handouts can be distributed either before or after the talk. If you distribute them before the talk, the audience can make notes on the handout, which is particularly helpful in decision-making contexts; the disadvantage in normal presentations is that the audience will be reading the handout rather than listening to you. Most presenters prefer to distribute handouts after the presentation, where it serves as a takeaway for the audience.

To Read or to Speak?

Experienced speakers can stand up and talk without benefit of notes or slides, and charismatic speakers can hold the attention of the audience for an hour. Most of us lose our way during a talk, forget points, stumble over numbers, and suffer from stage fright.

There are two tools that can help you through an oral presentation. You can read out a paper or you can rely on transparencies/slides.

- **Reading out a paper**. Some presenters write out the entire speech (including notes like 'Pause here') and then read it out to the audience. This helps nervous presenters who think they may forget what they have to say or do not want to look at the audience. Besides being boring, such a presentation is slow—people can read your paper faster than you can read it out loud.
- **Using transparencies or slides** (such as PowerPoint). You can write important or dense information on transparencies or slides, project them on a screen, and talk about the information. This method falls between a speech with no notes and reading an entire paper out loud. Important information is put on the slides so that the speaker does not forget them; at the same time, the speaker can talk in a natural manner about this information.

Preparation

The first and obvious step in preparing your presentation is to gather material. Once you have the material, what do you do with it?

First, think about your **audience**. Who is the talk for? How much do they know and much should they know? This decides the type and level of information that you provide.

Second, **organise** your information. Use index cards or PowerPoint to organise your points. You need to tell a coherent story.

Creating Slides

At this point you start thinking in terms of what the audience will see projected on a screen. You can use overhead transparencies or a software program like PowerPoint; it depends on the technology available to you. This section discusses how to use PowerPoint but many of the principles are similar to overhead transparencies.

Purpose of the slides

PowerPoint is useful for three reasons. First, your speech is backed up by text for listeners who prefer to read. Second, you don't have to remember information or read from a paper—the slides act as your map and a memory aid. But the most important reason is that you can project information that cannot be conveyed through speaking or text. You can embed and play audio files, video clips, animations and simulations. For example, in economics, you can show changes in a graph through simulations, and in communication skills, you can play a video of a scenario.

Designing the slides

The overarching rule is that your slides should be clear. Use a clear structure, bullets, and plenty of white space. The number of slides is roughly:

Introduction (1) + Organisation of the talk (1) + Body + Conclusion (1)

The bulk of the slides come in the Body and depends on the amount of time you have for your presentation.

Structuring the body of the talk presents problems peculiar to PowerPoint. The structure of the talk can get lost as one slide follows another similar-looking slide. The distinction between main points and sub-points is easily lost and the hierarchical structure gets flattened. To get over this problem, we use different layouts for main points and sub-points.

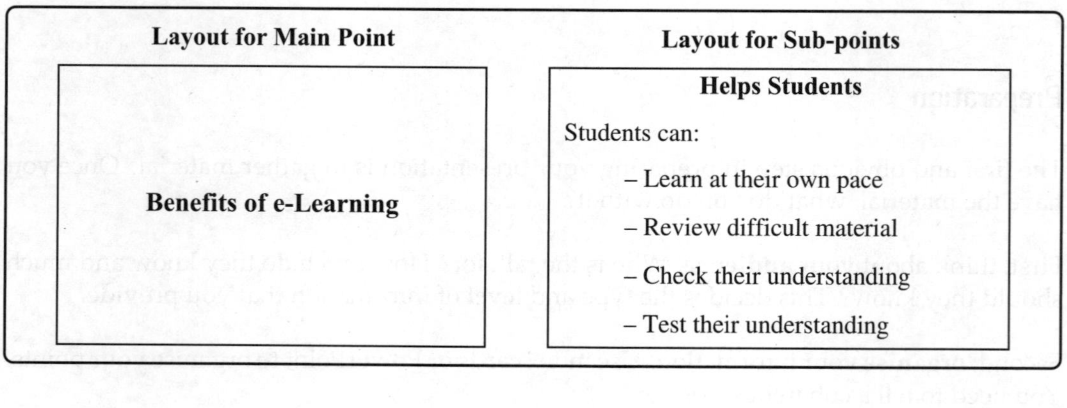

Displaying data

If you use any kind of data, you cannot merely talk about it; the audience needs an image or text that they can follow. Imagine trying to describe a graph that no one can see; it will make no sense.

Data that is displayed has another advantage, this one for the presenter. Instead of stumbling over complicated numbers, you can point to the slide and merely say, 'The numbers show...' or 'These are the dimensions'. The slides will give the audience the hard facts, freeing you to talk about the important aspects.

When you create a visual, select a format that is easy to understand. It is difficult to read tables fast, so, if possible, convert them into another format, such as a graph or a map. Below are two ways to show data: in a figure and as a table. Notice that it is easier to understand the image than to work your way through the numbers in the table.

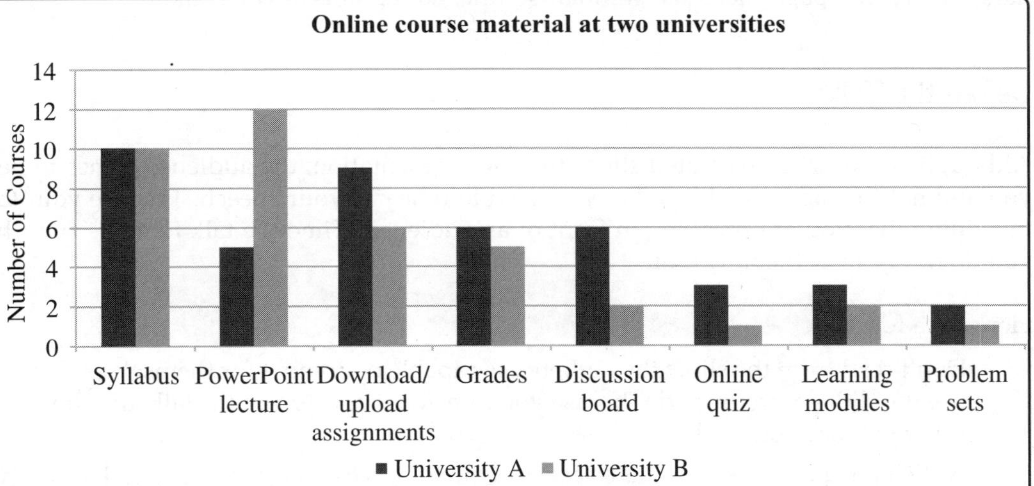

Figure 12.1: Data in a bar chat

Table12.1: Data in a table

Online material	**University A**	**University B**
Syllabus	10	10
PowerPoint lecture	5	12
Download/upload assignments	9	6
Grades	6	5
Discussion board	6	2

Online quix	3	1
Learning modules	3	2
Problem sets	2	1

Notes and handouts

If you really cannot do without a written text, you can make notes on a few index cards. Don't use too many index cards because they can get mixed up. In PowerPoint you can type your notes into the Notes section. When you print out this section, you will have a copy of each slide with the relevant notes for your talk.

As handouts, you can print out your slides (say, 6 slides on one page). A more useful handout is a one-page sheet that summarises the main points of your talk.

Before the Talk

Although you may have created slides for your presentation, the audience comes to hear you and not to read your slides. So, you need to rehearse your speech. Practise your talk imagining that you are speaking in front of an audience. Time the talk to make sure that you do not go over the time limit.

Here are a few tips.

- Don't read from the slide; the audience is capable of doing it for themselves. Instead, use the slides as your guide. In case you lose your way during the talk, the slides will bring you back on track.
- Anticipate questions you will be asked. One trick is to keep some material in reserve, so that you can dazzle the audience with your off-the-cuff brilliance.
- Your slides or transparencies should contain all the information you need. Add extra slides as a backup for questions that may come up.
- Be aware that you depend on technology, and if technology can fail, it will. The electricity may fail; another common glitch is that the computer may work but the projector may not. So, have a backup. Carry a printout and handouts. Carry a copy of your presentation on a thumb drive; you can also email the file to yourself if there are facilities to download it from the Internet at the other end.

On the Podium

A lot of people are nervous about doing an oral presentation because they have never spoken in front of an audience. We are more used to a system where 'Children should be seen and not heard' or 'The nail that sticks out will be hammered down.'

This is not a problem for two groups of people—teachers and actors. Teachers speak to groups every day of their working lives, and they enjoy it. This is because they are not focused on the impression they are making but on getting their message across. Actors are also comfortable speaking in public; if you are extremely nervous, imagine that you are acting on stage.

Before you begin your talk, take a deep breath, relax—and try to enjoy yourself.

Handling Questions

When your presentation is over, people will ask questions and you should be prepared for this. In fact, consider questions a compliment because this means that your presentation was interesting; it is disappointing not to be asked questions.

Think about questions you might be asked and prepare your answers. If you have planned well, you might even have prepared a slide on this and you can say, 'I have a slide here' as you move to that slide.

Another strategy is to save some information for the Q&A session. You cannot include everything in your presentation, so consider keeping some information in reserve that you can bring out in the Q&A session.

EXERCISES

Q1. As a manager in an e-Learning company, you have to prepare three presentations: (a) for the board of a school that is deciding whether to adopt e-Learning, (b) for teachers in a school that has adopted e-Learning, and (c) for your development team that will create the courses.

Here are some points you can use. What information will you use for each presentation?

- The history of computing and the Internet
- What is e-learning?
- Benefits for teachers
- Available tools—chat, discussion forum, email, etc.
- Budget estimate
- Specifications of the Learning Management System
- Development time for each module
- How to use e-Learning in class
- Benefits for administrators
- Profit for the company

Q2. Look at the slides below and identify the problem with each slide.

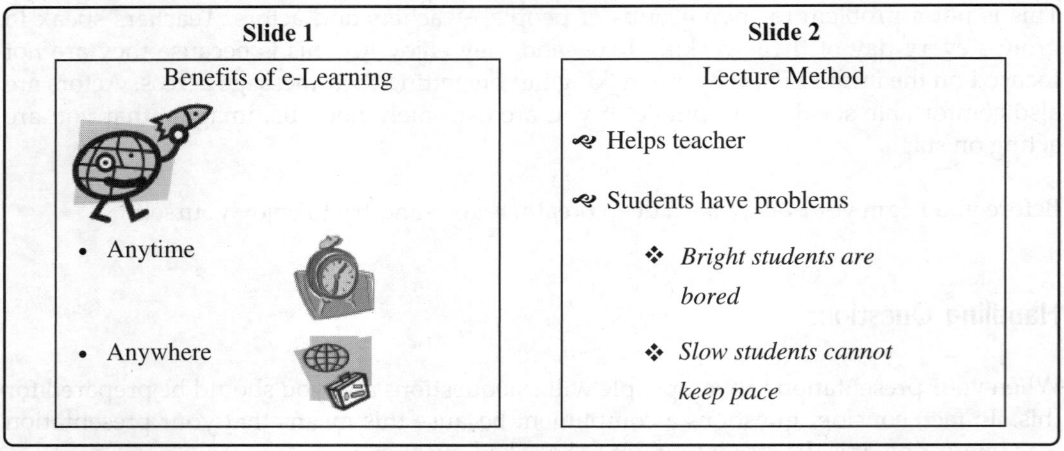

Q3. Here is the information that a presenter tried to fit on one slide. Use this information to create two slides.

- The main challenge facing universities lies not in the acquisition of technology or know-how but in creating content that is appropriate for both the courses and the technology.
- The current courses do not use the technology effectively or imaginatively, because they are still working with the traditional model of a teacher who explains the content to an audience of students sitting in a traditional classroom.
- As a result, the material is merely a digitised version of the textbook or a PowerPoint file using only text. Links to websites that give additional information are provided. In an attempt to use technology, the lecturer is videotaped lecturing the class, with students asking questions.
- Such uses of technology barely tap the potential of e-Learning.

Q4. Here is some information from a section of the talk. Create a set of slides for the audience. Remember to use brief phrases.

Although the initial expense for setting up e-Learning is enormous, educational institutions are turning to e-Learning for several reasons. The most obvious reason is that there is a limit to the physical space in universities and they cannot cope with increasing enrolment. Having more students requires more teachers that universities can ill afford, and e-Learning is a way to overcome these two physical constraints. Second, e-Learning provides access to up-to-date information, reducing the dependence on textbooks and finding super-qualified teachers. Students can access the latest information, leaving the teacher to focus on teaching rather than on content transmission. Finally, the quality of learning improves, because collaborative tools encourage students to construct knowledge instead of passively receiving information.

Q5. How would you handle the following? Someone in the audience:

1. Asks a question that is not clear.
2. Asks you a question you don't understand.
3. Asks a question to which you don't know the answer.
4. Asks why you have not covered another vast area in your presentation.
5. Launches into a lecture.
6. Starts attacking you and your presentation.

ANSWERS

1. (a) For administrators
    - What is e-learning?
    - Benefits for administrators
    - Benefits for teachers
    - Budget estimate

   (b) For teachers
    - What is e-learning?
    - Benefits for teachers
    - Available tools—chat, discussion forum, email, etc.
    - How to use e-Learning in class

   (c) For the development team
    - Specifications of the Learning Management System
    - Available tools—chat, discussion forum, email, etc.
    - Development time for each module

2. - **Graphics.** Do the pictures add anything to your points or are they there for 'interest'? Since PowerPoint allows you to insert pictures, people think this is a wonderful way to liven up text. However, pictures that are merely decoration distract from your message, undercut the seriousness of your talk, and can be downright annoying.
   - **Fonts.** How many fonts are you going to use? With so many fonts to choose from, there is a temptation to embellish your slide with different fancy fonts. Unfortunately, the text becomes unreadable. The best choice is Arial font.
   - **Long sentences**. The author has written out the entire text and probably plans to read it out to the audience. But the audience can read faster and will get impatient. Second, to fit in all the text, the font size has become so small that the audience cannot read it. It is better to use short phrases that the audience can read fast; then you can expand on the phrases and explain what you mean.

3.

Slide 3

Challenges for Universities

- The main challenge facing universities lies not in the acquisition of technology or know-how but in creating content that is appropriate for both the courses and the technology.
- The current courses do not use the technology effectively or imaginatively, because they are still working with the traditional model of a teacher who explains the content to an audience of students sitting in a traditional classroom.
- As a result, the material is merely a digitised version of the textbook or a PowerPoint file using only text. Links to websites that give additional information are provided. In an attempt to use technology, the lecturer is videotaped lecturing the class, with students asking questions.
- Such uses of technology barely tap the potential of e-Learning.

4.

Challenges for Universities

- To create content that exploits the technology

Problems with Current e-Learning Courses

- Use the traditional lecture method
- Courses are:
  - o digitised versions of the textbook
  - o PowerPoint files using only text
  - o videos of the teacher lecturing to a class

5. **Possible answers**

(a) Summarise the question to check if this is what the questioner wants to know. For example, say, 'Are you asking whether...?' Or 'Is your question...?'
(b) If you don't understand the question, ask for help from the audience. For example, you can say 'I'm afraid I don't understand the question. Could someone help?'
(c) If you don't know the answer, say so. 'I'm afraid I don't know but I'll look it up and let you know.' Or you can say, 'That's an interesting point I hadn't thought about' and start scribbling as if it is an important point.
(d) Say politely that this is beyond the scope of your talk.
(e) Faced with a lecture, interrupt and ask, 'Is that a question or a comment?' or 'What is your question?'
(f) Faced with an attack, turn to the moderator for help.

APPENDIX: SAMPLE FEEDBACK FORM

Feedback for Presenter		
Name of Presenter:		
Name of Evaluator:		
DELIVERY		
Eye contact	Good	Weak
Appropriate gestures	Good	Weak
Rate of speech	Good	Weak
Volume	Good	Weak
CONTENT		
Introduction	Good	Weak
Organisation	Good	Weak
Conclusion	Good	Weak
Visual aids	Good	Weak

CHAPTER 13

Beyond Grammar or Editing for Style

INTRODUCTION

When you have a draft of your paper, you should spend some time checking the language. Read through the paper to edit the sentences and words so that the ideas are easy to follow and the words convey exactly what you want to say. This goes beyond grammar and comes under style.

The language used in research articles and reports has been criticised for being abstract and dense. Some of this is necessary, but in many cases the writing can be made clearer and more accessible. Below are two examples.

Examples

1. However, before the grant of permanent registration that evidence submitted by the applicants of having complied with the standards would be displayed for the public at large for filing objections.
2. However, before permanent registration is granted, applicants should submit evidence that they have complied with the standards, which would then be displayed to the public for filing objections.

Sentence 1 is the kind of language that is found in bureaucratic prose and some research articles. Although it sounds impressive, it is difficult to understand. Sentence 2 is still dense but easier to follow.

In this chapter, we will look at single sentences and in the next chapter we turn to words and phrases. These two chapters do not deal with topic progression and information flow, or how we move from one sentence to the next in connected discourse; that discussion belongs in a more advanced course.

This chapter is confined to the following:

1. The basic sentence

2. Verbs: Empty verbs and delayed verbs
3. Nouns: Nominalisations and heavy noun phrases
4. Ending a sentence
5. Delayed Subjects: It, there, what
6. Long sentences
7. Short sentences
8. Parallelism

The Basic Sentence

Let's look at the structure of a basic sentence.

> An analysis of the data was done in two stages to identify the main effects.
> Noun Phrase + Verb + Adjunct

This sentence can be sharpened by replacing the weak verb *was done* with one of the nouns, *analysis*.

> The data was *analysed* in two stages to identify the main effects.

We can also move the phrase at the end to the beginning.

> T*o identify the main effects*, the data was analysed in two stages.

In the next three sections, we look at these three components of a basic sentence—the verbs, nouns and adjuncts—to see how they can be simplified. Briefly, in much of this prose, the verbs are merely placeholders, the nouns are abstract nouns, and the adjuncts make the sentence fade away. It is quite easy to fix some of the more obvious problems, which we look at below.

Verbs

Empty Verbs

Verbs are supposed to show action. However, verbs such as *be* merely show the existence or presence of something.

> The purpose of the pilot study *is* to identify likely candidates for the project.

Find a word in the sentence that can replace the verb *be*.

> The pilot study *identifies* likely candidates for the project.

Here are more verbs that merely take up space: *make*, *do*, *have*, *give*, and *get*. Often, they can be replaced with more active verbs. In the example below, we have taken a noun in the sentence and converted it into a verb.

Example: Great people have *made* contributions to society.

Solution: If possible, replace the verb with a noun from the sentence.

Answer: Great people have *contributed* to society.

Delayed Verbs

Unlike most languages, in English the verb comes in the middle of the sentence and not at the end. If the verb comes at the end of the sentence, readers have to hold a long noun phrase in their memory until they reach the verb.

Example
The scientific study of language and its structure *is called* linguistics.
Linguistics *is* the scientific study of language and its structure.

Nouns

Here we look at two potential problems when using nouns: excessive nominalisation and heavy noun phrases.

Nominalisations

In the section on empty verbs, we saw that we can replace a static verb by selecting a noun and converting it into a verb.

1. Since the requests were confidential, it is difficult to *make an assessment* of them.
2. Since the requests were confidential, it is difficult to *assess* them.

In Sentence 1, the noun *assessment* has been created from the verb *assess*. This is called *nominalisation* or making a noun. We simplify the sentence by turning the noun back into a verb, *assess*.

Here are more examples.

Verb	**Noun**
discover	discovery
move	movement
react	reaction

refuse	refusal
withdraw	withdrawal
discuss	discussion
fail	failure
pay	payment

As we saw in the previous section, these nouns are often introduced by empty verbs such as *make, do, give,* and *have* as well as *provide* and *perform.* Adjectives can also be nominalised.

Adjective	**Noun**
careless	carelessness
difficult	difficulty
different	difference
applicable	applicability

Nominalisation tends to fill the text with abstract nouns, making it difficult to understand.

Heavy Noun Phrase

Some noun phrases contain several nouns strung together. A phrase such as weighted risk capital allocation model is a technical term that should be retained. But in other cases, the noun phrase can be ambiguous or difficult to understand.

The solution is to break up the long noun phrase into smaller chunks with words like *of* and *in*; we can also use *that* and *by.* The revised sentence is longer, but clearer.

Examples

1. The organisation has started a school for migrant labourer children.
   Who are the migrants: the labourers or the children?
   The organisation has started a school for *the children of migrant labourers*.
2. The negotiations on developing country flexibilities broke down.
   Is it *flexibilities of developing countries* or do they want to *develop* the flexibilities of countries?
3. This scheme gives duty-free access to Sri Lanka-made garments.
   The noun phrase *Sri Lanka-made garments* is awkward. It can be replaced with a clearer phrase–garments made in Sri Lanka.
4. The institutional change-facilitating upgrading of domestic industrial structure and supplier capabilities leads to greater global trade participation.
   I give up.

Ending a Sentence

During reading, our eyes jump over words in the sentence and come to rest on the words before the full stop. The words at the end of a sentence receive the maximum attention during reading, so make sure that the words just before the full stop are important.

Example: Things change quickly and unpredictably in the world.

Solution: Move the phrase in the world to the beginning of the sentence.

Possible answer: In the world, things change quickly and unpredictably.

Delayed Subjects: It, There, and What

Look at the following set of sentences.

1. Mansi lived in Paris.
2. It was in Paris that Mansi lived (i.e., not in London or Mumbai)
3. It was Mansi who lived in Paris (i.e., not Sonali or Kartik)

In Sentences 2 and 3, one piece of information is emphasised, namely, the place or the person. This emphasis is provided by using *It* + *be* to begin the sentence.

Similarly, we can use *There* + *be* to provide emphasis.

1. The analysis can be done in two ways.
2. *There are* two ways in which the analysis can be done. (not in one or three ways)

Here is a third way to emphasise information, using *what*.

1. She wants to eat fish.
2. *What* she wants to eat is fish. (not vegetables or fruit)

Although these three techniques help you emphasise information, they make the sentence longer and more difficult to understand. So, unless you deliberately want to emphasise a part of the information, delete these extra words from your sentence.

The Long and Winding Sentence

To display their command of the language, many writers try to use long, complex sentences. Here is one sentence.

> The danger of long and complex sentences, with their numerous subordinate clauses that permit you to express your ideas in depth and complexity, with caveats, where necessary, allow you to display your mastery of the nuances of the language, and enable you to impress the reader, or the examiner, as the case may be with your linguistic ability, is that you may lose sight of the most basic rule in English sentence structure, namely, subject-verb agreement.

Go ahead and use complex sentences; but when you are done, find the head noun (*danger*) and the verb (*is*)—and make them match.

> **Example**
> Knowledge about the relationship between inflation and its determinants remain limited.
>
> The subject of the sentence is not *determinants;* it is *knowledge.* So, the verb (*remain*) must agree with *knowledge.* In a long sentence, you may have to hunt for the subject.
>
> Knowledge about the relationship between inflation and its determinants *remains* limited.

SHORT SENTENCES

Short sentences are good but too many short sentences are not good. They have a choppy effect. Combine short sentences into longer ones. This gives variety.

To combine sentences, find related ideas and use complex sentences or a semi-colon.

> **Example**
> The mixture is yellow and absorbs water. It has a boiling point of 60 degrees.
>
> **Solution:** The facts are related, so combine the sentences.
>
> **Possible answer:** The mixture is yellow, absorbs water, and has a boiling point of 60 degrees.

PARALLELISM

The following sentences are correct because the forms are parallel.

- Dev likes drawing cartoon characters and playing the drums. (gerunds)
- Dev likes to draw cartoon characters and to play the drums. (to + infinitive)

But don't mix the two forms. The sentence below is grammatically wrong because drawing is a gerund whereas to play is the infinitive form of the verb.

- Dev likes drawing cartoon characters and to play the drums.

Here is an example that shows how to use the two forms.

Incorrect: The programme assists schools in identifying their weaknesses and to select a development plan.

Correct: The programme assists schools in identifying their weaknesses and selecting a development plan.

Correct: The programme assists schools to identify their weaknesses and to select a development plan.

EXERCISES

Q1. In the sentences below, replace the verb with an action verb. You should be able to find a word in the sentence that can be converted into a verb.

1. The performance of the robot got stabilised after this.
2. We can come to the conclusion that foreign investors are interested in investing in this sector.
3. This foundation works in the field of primary education collaborating with the government.
4. Hospitals are making over-provision of healthcare services as well as giving inflated medical bills.
5. Since Ravi has obtained the support of the management, his focus should be placed on building his team.
6. The two committees have laid stress on the importance of teacher education.
7. We then made a differentiation between schools and universities.
8. The study also gives suggested measures for the functioning of the scheme.
9. Only a small percentage of people follow diet plans, which have a crucial role to play in overall health and well-being.
10. The case of the Three Gorges Dam in China provides a useful illustration of the disastrous consequences of large hydroelectric projects.
11. Any deviation from these guidelines would cause erosion of investor confidence.
12. The aim of these discussions was to get an understanding of the work being done by Indian healthcare providers.

Q2. Rewrite the sentences so that the verb comes towards the beginning of the sentence.

1. The subfield of computer science devoted to developing programs that enable computers to display behaviour that can be characterised as intelligent is called Artificial Intelligence.
2. Questions about the current textbook, teachers' familiarity with text genres, their views on teaching text genres in the middle school, etc. were also asked.
3. A strong distribution network, well-developed logistics, and intense competition characterise the consumer goods sector.
4. Growing consumer awareness, easier access to goods, and changing lifestyles are the main drivers of the consumer market.

Q3. In the sentences, below, identify the nominalisations. Simplify the sentences by converting the noun into a verb or adjective.

1. The confidence levels used in the computation need some revisions.
2. Recent advances in technology have resulted in a reduction in the size of mobile phones.
3. The committee was of the view that in the case of smaller schools, consolidation would be dependent on emerging market forces.
4. Much greater improvement has to take place in the Indian educational system before it is prepared to face competition from international institutions.
5. The assessment should cover whether there is retention of certain powers by the teachers.
6. With the development of the retail segment, there has been a proliferation of investment advisors.
7. The committee feels that the Labour Act may enable resolution of some of the operational issues.
8. The committee has recommended certain measures for the enhancement of student learning.
9. Given the discontinuation of the central government's loans for state plans, it may require an increase in states' recourse to market borrowings.
10. Guaranteed employment for farmers could reduce their debt, resulting in improvement in their financial situation and a reduction in their loan defaults.
11. As India is primarily an oil-importing country, oil prices constitute a critical element in the sustainability of the Indian growth process and the maintenance of financial stability.

Q4. In the sentences below, break up the heavy noun phrase.

1. The European Union has placed restrictions on data outsourcing on data security grounds.
2. The study suggests a portfolio performance evaluation measure.
3. Financial market participants' response to this liquidity squeeze was to reduce their exposure to all complex investments.
4. I will use three techniques for a comparison of these four mutual fund schemes' performance.
5. A too-detailed daily or long-term plan does not stimulate people's creative spirit and initiatives.

Q5.

1. The top-down method is better in this case.
2. Education plays an increasingly important role in society now.
3. We know that for any company the bottom line is sales and turnover and customers are the most important people to them.
4. There has been massive capital inflow in the form of FDI this year.
5. Risk in a mutual fund is based on fluctuations of the returns generated by it.
6. India and Japan can together play important roles in both Afghanistan and Myanmar, for example.

7. The commercial importance of the port stems from its potential to become an alternative energy supply route from the Middle East to western China in the end.

Q6. Where possible, make the sentence shorter and clearer by deleting the *it, what,* and *there* phrases.

1. It is the final product which determines the sales of the company.
2. When individuals harm the environment, it is the time for the government to protect it for the benefit of the public.
3. What has become clear is that Haiti's crisis is likely to deepen, with serious political, economic and humanitarian consequences.
4. What is striking is the high correlation between student motivation and test scores.
5. There are several instances where malnutrition has not been reported.
6. There are several areas that have been identified as critical to the success of education programmes.
7. It is estimated that India's small hydropower potential is around 15,000 MW.
8. There are two areas that are relevant to a discussion of student success. These relate to: (a) equity and (b) quality.
9. There are a lot of enquiries from Scandinavian countries about conducting clinical research and trials in India.

Q7. Here are some additional texts that could be simplified.

1. There is a need to accelerate the current level of investment in infrastructure from 5.0 per cent of GDP during 2006-07 to 9.0 per cent during the Plan period.
2. These are the markets that are likely to be compelled to open up their healthcare systems in the near future.
3. There has been little interest on the part of the EU to set up medical education campuses in India.
4. There are independent telemedicine providers engaged in providing telemedicine to other countries as well as reputed IT companies.
5. There are prescribed formats for submission of documents. There is a requirement for excessive documentation, such as the CV, work experience, teaching, administration, research, and college activities. The time taken to get the documentation together for the filing requirements may take three to four months. It may subsequently take two to three months for the queries raised by the council to be addressed, following the submission of documents. There is also a final requirement for the applicant to go in person and identify himself/herself for getting registered.

Q8.

1. That said, concluding trade negotiations have never been easy.
2. The construction of a port at the site of the turtle breeding grounds were opposed internationally.
3. The system of registration of security interest in respect of immovable property, motor vehicles, intellectual property and in respect of assets of companies provide adequate notice of creation of the security interest to the public.

4. The next section will discuss in brief the specifics of the Doha Round that has brought out the inconsistencies so much more starkly.
5. The supportive policy environment in terms of fiscal, trade, other incentives and targeted programmes for the industry, and a liberal foreign investment regime has led to a steady increase in inward foreign investment in India's IT-ITES sector.
6. Given that the dimensions of this turmoil and its impact both on the real economy and on the world of finance is still uncertain, this period represents a turnaround.
7. With the growing integration of the Indian economy with global markets, the weight of global factors, along with domestic considerations, have also become important in dictating macroeconomic policies and outcomes.
8. Given the high level of IT security systems and protocols in place in India's IT industry, restrictions on the outsourcing of data on data security grounds is not justified.
9. The panel has, however, identified a few areas in the equities market that requires focused attention.

Q9. The texts below consist of a series of short sentences and the relationships between the ideas are not clear. Try to combine the sentences so that the ideas are connected.

1. The study found that teachers support the introduction of inquiry-based learning. Most of them were not sure how to implement it in the classroom.
2. The main problem is the lack of infrastructure. Most of the centres are run in open spaces or private houses. Only 5–10% of the centres have their own building.
3. There is no duplication of efforts because of the simultaneous existence of creches and preschool centres. Creches and preschool centres perform different functions.
4. The efficiencies of coal power plants should be improved. This can be done by using better quality coal, upgrading the technology and implementing best management practices. For environmental reasons, power stations should be located at pit-heads. This will also reduce the high cost of transporting coal.

Q10. In the sentences below, check whether the constructions are parallel.

1. It increases the ability to adapt, enhances efficiency and create a more pleasant environment within the company.
2. International pharmaceutical companies are seeking an Indian presence and invest in India as a manufacturing base.
3. The recent decision by the state to withdraw from social sector spending and inviting more private players is a step forward.
4. Some countries have initiated reforms by undertaking quality assurance programmes, providing guarantees of reduced wait time, restructuring healthcare delivery, adopting IT strategies, and development of health plans for citizens.

Answers

1. (a) The performance of the robot stabilised.
   (b) We can conclude that foreign investors are interested in investing in this sector.
   (c) This foundation collaborates with the government in the field of primary education.
   (d) Hospitals over-provide healthcare services and inflate medical bills.
   (e) Since Ravi has obtained the support of the management, he should focus on building his team.
   (f) The two committees have stressed the importance of teacher education.
   (g) We then differentiated between schools and universities.
   (h) The study also suggests measures for the functioning of the scheme.
   (i) Only a small percentage of people follow diet plans, which play a crucial role in overall health and well-being.
   (j) The case of the Three Gorges Dam in China illustrates the disastrous consequences of large hydroelectric projects.
   (k) Any deviation from these guidelines would erode investor confidence.
   (l) These discussions aimed to understand the work being done by Indian healthcare providers.

2. (a) Artificial Intelligence is a subfield of computer science devoted to developing programs that enable computers to display behaviour that can be characterised as intelligent.
   (b) Teachers were also asked questions about the current textbook, their familiarity with text genres, and their views on teaching text genres in the middle school.
   (c) The consumer goods sector is characterised by a strong distribution network, well-developed logistics, and intense competition.
   (d) The main drivers of the consumer market are growing consumer awareness, easier access to goods, and changing lifestyles.

3. (a) The confidence levels used in the computation need to be revised.
   (b) Recent advances in technology have reduced the size of mobile phones.
   (c) The committee felt that consolidation of the smaller schools would depend on emerging market forces.
   (d) The Indian educational system has to be improved before it can compete with international institutions.
   (e) The assessment should cover whether teachers will retain certain powers.
   (f) With the development of the retail segment, investment advisors have proliferated.
   (g) The committee feels that the Labour Act may resolve some of the operational issues.
   (h) The committee has recommended certain measures to enhance student learning.
   (i) Since the central government has discontinued loans for state plans, the states may need to increase their market borrowings.

(j) Guaranteed employment for farmers could reduce their debt, thereby improving their financial situation and reducing their loan defaults.

(k) As India is primarily an oil-importing country, oil prices constitute a critical element in sustaining the Indian growth process and maintaining financial stability.

4. (a) The European Union has placed restrictions on data outsourcing on the grounds of data security.
   (b) The study suggests an evaluation measure for portfolio performance.
   (c) The response by financial market participants to this liquidity squeeze was to reduce their exposure to all complex investments.
   (d) I will use three techniques to compare the performance of these four mutual fund schemes.
   (e) A daily or long-term plan that is too detailed does not stimulate people's creative spirit and initiatives.

5. (a) In this case, the top-down method is better.
   (b) Now, education plays an increasingly important role in society.
   (c) We know that for any company the bottom line is sales and turnover and customers are the most important people.
   (d) This year there has been massive capital inflow in the form of FDI.
   (e) Risk in a mutual fund is based on fluctuations of the returns it generates.
   (f) For example, India and Japan can together play important roles in both Afghanistan and Myanmar.
   (g) The commercial importance of the port stems from its potential to eventually become an alternative energy supply route from the Middle East to western China.

6. (a) The final product determines the sales of the company.
   (b) When individuals harm the environment, the government should protect it for the benefit of the public.
   (c) Haiti's crisis is likely to deepen, with serious political, economic and humanitarian consequences.
   (d) The high correlation between student motivation and test scores is striking.
   (e) In several instances malnutrition has not been reported.
   (f) Several areas have been identified as critical to the success of education programmes.
   (g) India's small hydropower potential is around 15,000 MW.
   (h) Two areas relevant to a discussion of student success are: (a) equity and (b) quality.
   (i) Scandinavian countries have enquired about conducting clinical research and trials in India.

7. (a) The current level of investment in infrastructure needs to be accelerated from 5.0 per cent of GDP during 2006-07 to 9.0 per cent during the Plan period.
   (b) These markets may be compelled to open up their healthcare systems in the near future.

(c) The EU has shown little interest in setting up medical education campuses in India.

(d) Independent telemedicine providers as well as reputed IT companies provide telemedicine to other countries.

(e) The process involves excessive documentation (such as a detailed CV) that must be submitted in a prescribed format. It can take 3-4 months to gather the documentation and another 2-3 months to address the queries raised by the Council. Finally, to get registered the applicant must go in person and identify himself/herself.

8. (a) That said, concluding trade negotiations has never been easy.

(b) The construction of a port at the site of the turtle breeding grounds was opposed internationally.

(c) The system of registration of security interest in respect of immovable property, motor vehicles, intellectual property and in respect of assets of companies provides adequate notice of creation of the security interest to the public.

(d) The next section will discuss in brief the specifics of the Doha Round that have brought out the inconsistencies so much more starkly.

(e) The supportive policy environment in terms of fiscal, trade, other incentives and targeted programmes for the industry, and a liberal foreign investment regime have led to a steady increase in inward foreign investment in India's IT-ITES sector.

(f) Given that the dimensions of this turmoil and its impact both on the real economy and on the world of finance are still uncertain, this period represents a turnaround.

(g) With the growing integration of the Indian economy with global markets, the weight of global factors, along with domestic considerations, has also become important in dictating macroeconomic policies and outcomes.

(h) Given the high level of IT security systems and protocols in place in India's IT industry, restrictions on the outsourcing of data on data security grounds are not justified.

(i) The panel has, however, identified a few areas in the equities market that require focused attention.

9. (a) Although the study found that teachers support the introduction of inquiry-based learning, most of them were not sure how to implement it in the classroom.

(b) The main problem is the lack of infrastructure. Most of the centres are run in open spaces or private houses and only 5–10% of the centres have their own building.

(c) Since creches and preschool centres perform different functions, there is no duplication of efforts.

(d) The efficiencies of coal power plants should be improved by using better quality coal, upgrading the technology and implementing best management practices. Power stations should be located at pit-heads for environmental reasons and to reduce the high cost of transporting coal.

10. (a) It increases the ability to adapt, enhances efficiency and creates a more pleasant environment within the company.

(b) International pharmaceutical companies are seeking an Indian presence and are investing in India as a manufacturing base.

(c) The recent decision by the state to withdraw from social sector spending and to invite more private players is a step forward.

(d) Some countries have initiated reforms by undertaking quality assurance programmes, providing guarantees of reduced wait time, restructuring healthcare delivery, adopting IT strategies, and developing health plans for citizens.

CHAPTER

14

Working with Words

INTRODUCTION

In Chapter 8, we looked at the language of reports and research articles, and noted that these genres use formal language. But formal language does not mean using 'big words'. It means using words that your readers can understand without running to a dictionary, and using words that precisely and clearly express what you want to say.

Studies of the language in texts show that 21st century writing uses words that are short and precise; *Amongst* and *whilst* have given way to *among* and *while.* Expressions such as *He has rendered yeoman service* sound impressive but not many people know what it means. This change has occurred because the focus has shifted from beautiful expression to communicating with people in a hurry; as part of the Plain English movement, governments now realise that they have to communicate their vision and laws to their citizens in language that can be understood by the general public rather than lawyers. They now have a communications department that turns bureaucratic phrases such as *in pursuance of this matter* into *further*.

Precision in language is critical for academics, because they need to express their stance towards the studies they cite and their confidence in the data. Do they agree with the findings of the researchers? Do the findings merely suggest or do they firmly establish? Academics indicate their stand through the use of hedges (*suggest*) and emphatics (*definitely*).

This chapter does not try to build your vocabulary. Instead, it tries to make you look carefully at the words you have used. Are there stock phrases? Will your reader understand them? The sections are organised under different heads and you can go through them in any order.

1. Misleading words
2. Bureaucratic language
3. Replacing many words with one word
4. Complicated words

5. Avoiding metaphors
6. Redundant words
7. Expressing the degree of certainty
8. Capitalising words
9. Avoiding sexist language

MISLEADING WORDS

Some words and phrases may not be understood by an international audience. In other cases, writers use a word or phrase incorrectly.

Examples

- The banking sector has not been impacted *majorly*. *Majorly* is not an English word.
- The plan is assessed at *periodical* intervals.
  A periodical is a magazine. The correct word is *periodic*.

Bureaucratic Language

Bureaucratic prose is full of terms such as *deemed, as per* and *in accordance with.* We may not understand them but they are probably necessary because government documents need to be precise. However, if the document is to be read by the public, the language should be made readable; this has become imperative as governments all over the world try to communicate their visions and laws to their citizens. Reports that draw on government documents also need to modify the language for a general audience, but many reports use verbatim phrases from these documents.

ONE WORD FOR MANY

A single word is often as good as a long phrase. Instead of *for the reason that,* you can just say *because.* The table below gives a list of phrases that can be replaced by single words.

Phrase	Word
• for the reason that • owing to • due to the fact that, in light of the fact that, considering the fact that, on the grounds that, this is why	• because • since • why

• on the occasion of, in a situation in which, under circumstances in which,	• when
• it is crucial that • it is necessary that, there is a need/necessity for	• must • should
• is able to, has the opportunity to, has the capacity for, has the ability to	• can
• it is possible that • there is a chance that • the possibility exists for, there is a likelihood of	• may • might • could

Complicated Words

Borrowed Terms

Long, complicated words may sound impressive but your reader may not know them. More importantly, you may not know what they mean. The sentence below illustrates these two problems.

The use of the resources is in direct *proportionality* with the growth prospects.

Proportionality is a technical term in mathematics that means *having to do with proportion*, but the writer merely means *proportion*.

The use of the resources is in direct *proportion* to the growth prospects.

Noun + Noun Phrases

English allows one to create chunks such as *chicken soup*, where both words are nouns. Unfortunately, someone somewhere decided that the first noun should be an adjective, and so we get complicated phrases such as *agricultural sector*.

Avoiding Metaphors

In an effort to liven up dry prose, some writers include metaphors. However, metaphors do not translate well across cultures. For instance, the sentences below draw on archaic customs that have no relevance in a democratic age. They are a good way to exclude your reader from understanding your ideas.

- New players *don the mantle* of leadership.
- These countries are regular invitees to the negotiating *high table.*

Metaphors also send strong messages.

- These negotiations seem to be *paying lip service* to development concerns.

Paying lip service is strong condemnation. The author might want to tone it down with a less fiery phrase such as *token gesture* .

Metaphors are also difficult to handle. Writers sometimes use two metaphors, resulting in an odd image.

a The *fruits* were *reflected* in the leadership position it assumed.
Fruits as well as a mirror?

b The government has been given a *blanket clean chit.*
A huge blanket as well as a tiny chit?

Redundant Words

In speech, we often use redundant words because listeners may not catch them the first time. However, we do not need redundancy in written texts because readers can backtrack and re-read what they have missed. In fact, redundant words in written texts are annoying and take up space.

> Often, writers (frequently) do not re-read their texts (again) to remove (and eliminate) repeated and redundant ideas (and concepts). When you (completely) finish writing your paper, focus (particularly) on the words, and delete (or remove) any words that are opaque (and non-transparent). The (final) outcome will be a clear text (that readers can easily understand).

There are several types of redundant words, but four categories are covered below: (a) subset of a category, (b) repeated meaning, (c) unnecessary explanation and (d) redundant prepositions.

Subset of a Category

In the example below, small is a size and light is a weight.

> A smartphone is *small in size* and *light in weight.*

We would re-write this as below.

> A smartphone is small and light.

Redundant Pairs

We have heard or seen these phrases so often that it does not strike us that they contain redundant information.

> The *end result* is that no organisation can work effectively.

Since we get results at the end and not the beginning, delete *end*.

> The *result* is that no organisation can work effectively.

Redundant Prepositions

The verbs *say* and *talk* are straightforward, but their synonyms may contain a preposition. For example, take the word *discuss*, which means *talk about*. We can say, 'Let's talk about...', but we cannot say 'Let's discuss about...' because we are saying, *talk about about*.

Downright Wrong

The following phrases seem to have crept into written English. Think about why they are incorrect. Hint: How do we mark the comparative degree?

1. more stronger
2. lesser than
3. more faster

Unnecessary Explanation

Sometimes, terms and phrases need to be explained, but often explanations are unnecessary and merely add length (and wind) to a sentence.

> **Examples**
> Detailed daily and long-term plans can give us *a direction where we want to go*.
>
> *Direction* and *where we want to go* mean the same.

Expressing the Degree of Certainty

Here is a conversation between a customer and an employee at a telecom centre.

> Customer: Why is my SIM card not working?
> Employee: The SIM card has got corrupted....Your previous provider did not update the SIM card....Our electronic device did not accept your personal details.
> Customer: You have given me three explanations. Which one is it?

The problem here is that the employee offers three reasons as facts rather than as possibilities. He should have said:

> Employee: The SIM card *may* have got corrupted.... *Perhaps* your previous provider did not update the SIM card.... It is *possible* that our electronic device did not accept your personal details.

Words like *may, perhaps* and *possible* indicate that the speaker is not sure about the accuracy of the information. These are called *hedges.*

When the employee is certain, he uses an *emphatic.*

> Employee: I've checked our database. It is *definitely* a problem with our electronic device.

Encyclopaedias and dictionaries provide established facts, so they do not need to hedge or emphasise content. But in research papers and reports, the information may be debatable—some researchers hold one point of view, whereas others have a different opinion. Words like *perhaps* and *certainly* signal how confident the writer is about the accuracy of the information.

Notice what the table shows. First, there are more hedges than emphatics; in a complete list, the proportion of hedges is even larger. This is because we are wary of committing when we write.Take a sentence like the following.

> Private colleges charge exorbitant fees.

This would raise questions like the following.

- Do 100% of private colleges charge exorbitant fees? Are there any exceptions?
- How much is considered exorbitant? Twice the norm or 20 times the norm? Who considers it exorbitant—poor applicants, all applicants, the writer?

A careful writer would qualify this statement with hedges.

> *Most* private colleges charge *high* fees.

Also, the table includes the modals *could, will* and *must* as examples, but there are more modal verbs–*can, may, might, shall, should, would, must,* The primary function of modals is to indicate modality, which is the opinion and judgement of the speaker or writer about a statement. They are used to indicate possibility, probability, desire, necessity, obligation, etc. In the sentences below, the modal verb changes the meaning of the sentence.

- The course includes problem sets. Neutral.
- The course *might* include problem sets. Possibility.
- The course *should* include problem sets. Suggestion.
- The course *must* include problem sets. Obligation.

Modal verbs are used heavily in academic writing to indicate the author's stand. Most often, writers prefer to hedge rather than to commit. One rarely finds *must* in an academic paper.

Hedges

We use hedges or qualifiers when we do not want to commit or are unsure. Research articles make extensive use of hedges, because the readers are experts; the writer does not speak from a position of authority but has to establish his or her credibility. Hedges deflect criticism by toning down the strength of the claim, allowing other points of view, and providing room for negotiation.

However, hedges can be overused because the writer is trying to be careful. When we finish writing a paper, we usually go through it once to delete extra hedges.

Emphatics

Emphatics are words and phrases such as *obviously, certainly* and *of course*. Emphatics should be used with care and only when you are certain about the claim. They can make your claims sound extreme, undercut your credibility, and alienate your readers. Avoid strong adjectives and, instead, add qualifiers such as *often* or *most*.

Mixing Hedges and Emphatics

If you do not pay attention to the purpose of hedges and emphatics, you might end up sending mixed signals that confuse the reader. In the following sentence, the degree of certainty is not clear because both hedges and emphatics have been used.

> I'm *sure* the government *might* implement the plan.

CAPITALISATION

Some students are taught to capitalise important words so that they stand out for the examiner.

> Hydro-electric power can be effective in the following sectors of the state economy—*Agriculture, Fibre Processing, Tourism*, etc.

This is unnecessary, because we have other devices, such as bold and italics, to do the job. Capital letters also make reading difficult, so use them only when essential.

Some rules for capitalisation are obvious. Use capital letters—

a) To begin a sentence

- The committee prepared a draft.

b) For abbreviations

- NCERT

c) For proper nouns

- See Figure 3. The figure shows....

In all other cases, please avoid capital letters.

Sexist Languages

By convention, English titles use the masculine form. The male pronoun was also used as a generic term to refer to humans. This kind of language creates problems today. For example, organisations are run by a chairman, but what if the chairman is female? The solution is to use a gender-neutral term such as *chairperson*. Does it matter? The bias doesn't even occur to most men; in fact, they are puzzled when they manage to offend most of their colleagues (given the rising numbers of women in the workplace).

But there is a further problem.

> According to university regulations, every professor must provide accurate information about his academic qualifications.
> Are female professors allowed to provide inaccurate information?
>
> Every student must bring his notebook.
> Can the girls leave their notebooks at home?

To avoid these problems, we use gender-neutral language in writing. This creates some tortured prose as we work with forms like *s/he* and *her/him*. One solution is to use the plural. We can say, '*Students* must bring *their* notebooks.'

Exercises

Q1. Each sentence contains a word or phrase that is either incorrect by international standards or is misleading. Identify the words/phrases.

a) The postal department plans an upgradation of its technology.
b) Dr. Rao passed out from Best Institute in 1999.
c) Commodities are costlier this week.
d) Certain organisations presently function as trade and industry associations.
e) Until and unless the court passes an order, the company is free to deal with its properties.
f) One way to get away with the problem is to use multiple tests.
g) In the last decade, exports have increased.
h) The graph shows that prices of commodities were vibrating during August.
i) This will lead to a vicious cycle of improvements in infrastructure.
j) The study does not take account of ground realities.

Q2. Find plain English equivalents for the phrases below.

(a) prior to (b) purchase (c) regarding (d) accorded (e) persons (f) in respect of (g) in the event of (h) in accordance with

Q3. Rewrite these phrases for the general public.

a) The foremost reason for this is
b) Many academics are of the opinion
c) There are many problems with primary education as it stands today.
d) In the first four months itself, the funds were spent.
e) Private equity investments are in the good interest of Indian companies.
f) It was deemed necessary to examine the regulations.
g) The study sought to examine these factors in depth.

Q4. Replace the phrases with appropriate words.

a) Sales of bottled mineral water have increased due to the fact that potable water is not readily available.
b) There is a necessity for the government to act on this matter.
c) If it is implemented, this programme has the capacity to generate income for the rural poor.
d) With regard to the stress test, the results were not clear.
e) We examined the ways in which the structures of the two chemicals differ.

Q5. The sentences below have borrowed technical terms from other disciplines, but they are used incorrectly. Replace the terms with their simpler forms.

a) This has led to a dualistic labour market structure.
b) At the meeting, the specificities of the proposal were discussed.
c) India must reduce its dependency on oil.
d) This depends on several conditionalities.

Q6. Look at the adjectives below. Is a noun better?

a) Non-governmental organisations
b) The government is examining the development of infrastructural facilities.
c) The informational gaps need to be filled.

Q7. Rewrite the sentences using neutral words to replace the metaphors.

a) Inflation has been a difficult beast to control in the past decade.
b) These principles are enshrined in the WTO.
c) There was a red carpet welcome for the Prime Minister.
d) The public sector has the lion's share of the Indian health insurance market.
e) Haiti requested humanitarian aid to the tune of US$510 million after the earthquake.
f) This is necessary to ensure a safe landing for the negotiations between the two countries.

Additional Practice

Here are more texts that could be written in simpler language.

a) The need of the hour is to modernise and diversify the agriculture sector. The government needs to ensure that economic progress is not sacrificed at the altar of short-term populism. Instead, the call of the day is to push through economic reforms.
b) The purpose is to rattle an indifferent government out of its state of perpetual slumber and to resist the onward march of globalisation.

Q8. In the phrases below, delete the general category if it is redundant.

a) various differences
b) often times
c) economics field
d) of a strange type
e) unusual in nature

Q9. In the phrases below, delete words that repeat an idea.

a) extend this forward
b) future plans
c) return back
d) the goal we wish to achieve
e) continue in the future

Q10. Here are some phrases. Look up the meaning of the verb and then see if the preposition should be added.

a) emphasise on
b) stress on
c) despite of
d) comprise of
e) request for

Q11. a) This scheme would make a significant difference if one were able to find the required faculty to teach in them.
b) We need laws made by the government to protect this public area.
c) It is difficult to make a concise and efficient plan for the things that will happen in the following days.
d) Healthcare providers should be classified into various categories.
e) The company was bankrupt because it was in the red.

Q12. Edit the following sentences by deleting words that repeat information.

a) A separate regime for banks and other financial institutions is very vital.
b) The boom in the IT sector is due to the efforts of private entrepreneurs.

c) Overlapping issues in regulation need to be clarified more fully.
d) Payments will subsequently taper off in the later stages.
e) Since the village is small, you can directly approach the Gram Panchayat to seek solutions to problems.
f) The current economic and financial crisis in the industrialised world has generated conservatism today.
g) There has been strong Japanese support for India to join the East Asian Summit and strong backing from Japan for a larger ASEAN+6 group.
h) Initially, they had a bad start.

Q13. The texts below contain unnecessary words. Try to delete redundant information. You may need to re-write the sentences.

a) Often the constraints faced are not due to external regulations.
b) The questionnaire was designed to help in assisting policy co-ordination within the government. The questions asked whether this phenomenon is cyclical in nature.
c) The department faces losses due to defaults in receipt of payments from end-users.
d) In most public sector hospitals, the doctors and staff are rudely behaved.
e) When the tests were repeated again, similar results were obtained.
f) The price of cement and steel are calculated and then merged together.
g) By innovating new strategies, universities can deal with the faculty shortage.
h) There are guidelines and regulatory norms laid down that have to be followed.

Q14. Sort the words below into hedges and emphatics.

a) Verbs: appear, indicate, show
b) Nouns: claim, assumption, suggestion
c) Modals: could, must, will
d) Adverbs: clearly, possibly, likely
e) Adjectives: probable, possible, clear
f) Degree: approximately, all, often

Q15. In the sentences below, delete any extra hedges.

a) It seems as if it might safely be said that such radical ideas are likely to be ignored.
b) Such a heavy curriculum would have to be necessarily reduced.
c) It may be said without much exaggeration that diplomatic ties between the two countries have not quite followed a predictable track.
d) It may perhaps be expected that the workers will have additional demands.

Q16. In the sentences below, identify the emphatics. Re-write the sentences to make them more neutral.

a) There is no information available on the number of childcare institutions in India.

b) The financial crisis of the late 1990s and the collapse of the Internet bubble changed the Asian private equity industry forever.
c) At an annual growth rate of 8–9 percent, India is surely ahead of the developing economies.
d) There is a total lack of compassion and co-operation in these schools.
e) It is without doubt far more feasible than an FTA between China and India at the present stage.

Q17. In the sentences below, identify the hedges and intensifiers.

a) The survey found that the district schools are in a shocking state. Some schools are mere storage centres for grain and teachers' salaries are extremely low. This can definitely be considered a total failure of the educational system and one that the government may need to address.
b) A good plan always includes some contingency plans as a back-up.
c) The government seems to be quite keen to project the state as a model in which education has succeeded.
d) The building was raised at stupendous cost and effort.
e) There was a huge slashing of prices in 2016 compared to prices in 2011.
f) Today, many large multinational companies tend to do all their manufacturing in less developed countries where labour is cheap.
g) This seems typical of the state of primary and secondary schools in India.

Q18. In the sentences below, check whether the capital letters have been used correctly.

a) The Oil and natural gas commission was set up for exploration and drilling of Oil and Gas.
b) The data is given in table 2. From the Table it is clear that Exports to the EU increased in the past decade.
c) According to a circular issued by the government of India, the Government will provide funds for the Project.
d) The completion of the on-going negotiations on the comprehensive economic partnership agreement (CEPA) is expected to enhance Japan-India investment relations.
e) See annex 2 (table 1) for FDI stock by region in detail.

Q19. Change the sentence below so that the language is gender-neutral.

A person can have unlimited wealth in terms of property and money, but if *he* is not sure how *he* is going to use it, it becomes difficult for *him* to maintain *his* wealth.

ANSWERS

1. (a) The postal department plans to *upgrade* its technology.
Upgradation is not an English word, even though computer programmers think it is.

(b) Dr. Rao *graduated* from Best Institute in 1999.
Pass out means to faint or become unconscious. We normally used the generic word *graduate*.

(c) Commodities are *more expensive* this week.
When the price is high, we use *expensive*. Save *costly* for cases where you mean that there is a loss as in 'Delays in clinical trials can be costly for a pharmaceutical company'.

(d) *At present,* certain organisations function as trade and industry associations.
Presently means *soon*, but the writer wants to say *now*. For example, we would say, 'At present, there are no safeguards, but they will presently be put in place'.

(e) *Unless and until* the court passes an order, the company is free to deal with its properties.
In terms of logic, *if* (unless) comes before *when* (until).

(f) One way to *avoid* the problem is to use multiple tests.
To *get away with* means *not get caught*.

(g) In the *past* decade, exports have increased.
Last decade can be confusing. Is it the last decade of the 20th century (1989–1999) or is it the decade up to the time of writing (2007–2017)? *Past* means *previous*, and so *past decade* clearly refers to 2007–2017.

(h) The graph shows that prices of commodities were *fluctuating* during August.
Fluctuating is a technical term to describe trends in graphs. It cannot be replaced by a general word like *vibrating*.

(i) This will lead to a *virtuous cycle* of improvements in infrastructure.
A vicious cycle describes negative effects but improvements are not negative. The phrase *virtuous cycle* has been coined to describe positive effects.

(j) The study does not take account of *realities on the ground*.
Ground realities seems to be used only in India. The standard phrase is *realities on the ground*.

2. (a) before (b) buy (c) about (d) given (e) people (f) for (g) if (h) under

3. (a) The *main* reason is
(b) Many academics *think*
(c) There are many problems with primary education *today*.
(d) *Within* the first four months, the funds were spent.
(e) Private equity investments are in the *interest* of Indian companies.
(f) *We decided* to examine the regulations.
(g) The study *tried* to examine these factors in depth.

4. (a) Sales of bottled mineral water have increased *because* potable water is not readily available,
(b) The government *must* act on this matter.
(c) If it is implemented, this programme *can* generate income for the rural poor.
(d) The results of the stress test were not clear.
(e) We examined *how* the structures of the two chemicals differ.

5. (a) This has led to a *dual* labour market structure.
Dualistic is not an English word.

(b) At the meeting, the *specifics* of the proposal were discussed.
(c) India must reduce its *dependence* on oil.
(d) This depends on several *conditions*.

6. (a) Non-*government* organisations
(b) The government is examining the development of *infrastructure* facilities.
(c) The *information* gaps need to be filled.

7. (a) It has been difficult to control inflation in the past decade.
(b) These principles are protected in the WTO
(c) The Prime Minister was given a warm welcome.
(d) The public sector has the major share of the Indian health insurance market.
(e) Haiti requested US$510 million as humanitarian aid after the earthquake.
(f) This is necessary to ensure the success of the negotiations between the two countries.

8. (a) differences
(b) often
(c) economics
(d) strange
(e) unusual

9. (a) extend this
(b) plans
(c) return
(d) the goal
(e) continue

There are numerous other stock phrases where we do not notice that the words are redundant pairs. Here is a random list.

(a) past memories
(b) each individual
(c) basic fundamentals
(d) true facts
(e) actual facts
(f) important essentials
(g) terrible tragedy
(h) final outcome
(i) free gift
(j) past history
(k) unexpected surprise
(l) sudden crisis

11. (a) This scheme would make a significant difference if one were able to find the required faculty.
It is the job of faculty to teach.

(b) We need laws to protect this public area.
Laws are made by the government.

(c) It is difficult to make a concise and efficient plan.
Plan implies what will happen in the future.

(d) Healthcare providers should be classified.
Classifying implies categories.

(e) The company was bankrupt.
Bankrupt and *in the red* are synonyms.

12. (a) A separate regime for banks and other financial institutions is vital.
Something is either vital or it is not, so you don't need very. The same is true of words like *critical, crucial* and *exclusive.*

(b) The boom in the IT sector is due to the efforts of entrepreneurs.
Have you heard of a public entrepreneur?

(c) Overlapping issues in regulation need to be clarified.
Clarified means *made clear.*

(d) Payments will subsequently taper off.
Subsequently and *in the later stages* mean the same.

(e) Since the village is small, you can directly approach the Gram Panchayat with your problems.
Solutions imply that there is a problem.

(f) The current economic and financial crisis in the industrialised world has generated conservatism.
Current and *today* mean the same.

(g) There has been strong Japanese support for India to join the East Asian Summit and for a larger ASEAN+6 group.
Strong Japanese support covers both cases. You need to use it only once.

(h) They had a bad start.
Initially and *start* mean the same.

14.

	Hedges	**Emphatics**
Verbs	appear, indicate	show
Nouns	claim, assumption, suggestion	
Modals	could	will, must
Adverbs	possibly, likely	clearly
Adjectives	probable, possible	clear
Degree	approximately, often	all

15. (a) It might safely be said that such radical ideas are likely to be ignored.

(b) Such a heavy curriculum would have to be reduced.

(c) It may be said without exaggeration that diplomatic ties between the two countries have not followed a predictable track.

(d) It may be expected that the workers will have additional demands.

16. (a) There is *little* information available on the number of childcare institutions in India.
    (b) The financial crisis of the late 1990s and the collapse of the Internet bubble changed the Asian private equity industry.
    (c) At an annual growth rate of 8–9 percent, India is ahead of *most* developing economies.
    (d) There is a *general* lack of compassion and co-operation in these schools.
    (e) It is more feasible than an FTA between China and India at the present stage.

17. (a) The survey found that the district schools are in a *shocking* state. Some schools are *mere* storage centres for grain and teachers' salaries are *extremely* low. This can *definitely* be considered a *total* failure of the educational system and one that the government *may* need to address.
    (b) A good plan *always* includes some contingency plans as a back-up.
    (c) The government *seems* to be *quite* keen to project the state as a model in which education has succeeded.
    (d) The building was raised at *stupendous* cost and effort.
    (e) There was a *huge slashing* of prices in 2016 compared to prices in 2011.
    (f) Today, *many* big multinational companies *tend* to do *all* their manufacturing in less developed countries where labour is cheap.
    (g) This *seems* typical of the state of primary and secondary schools in India.

18. (a) The *Oil and Natural Gas Commission* was set up for exploration and drilling of *oil* and *gas.*
    (b) The data is given in *Table* 2. From the *table* it is clear that *exports* to the EU increased in the past decade.
    (c) According to a circular issued by the *Government of India,* the *government* will provide funds for the *project.*
    (d) The completion of the on-going negotiations on the *Comprehensive Economic Partnership Agreement* (CEPA) is expected to enhance Japan-India investment relations.
    (e) See *Annex* 2 (*Table* 1) for FDI stock by region in detail.

19. *People* can have unlimited wealth in terms of property and money, but if *they* are not sure how *they* are going to use it, it becomes difficult for *them* to maintain *their* wealth.

NOTES:

NOTES:

NOTES: